American Woodworker

HOW TO MAKE
Outdoor & Garden Furniture

D0731643

Published by Fox Chapel Publishing Company, Inc., 1970 Broad St., East Petersburg, PA 17520,
717-560-4703, *www.FoxChapelPublishing.com*

American Woodworker, ISSN 1074-9152, USPS 738-710, is published bimonthly by Woodworking Media, LLC,
90 Sherman St., Cambridge, MA 02140, *www.AmericanWoodworker.com*.

Library of Congress Control Number:
ISBN-13: 978-1-56523-765-0
ISBN-10: 1-56523-765-X

Library of Congress Cataloging-in-Publication Data

How to make outdoor & garden furniture / editor, American woodworker magazine.
    pages cm
  Includes index.
  ISBN 978-1-56523-765-0
  1. Outdoor furniture. 2. Woodwork. I. American woodworker. II. Title: How to make outdoor and garden furniture.
  TT197.5.O9H69 2012
  645'.8--dc23
                            2012030377

To learn more about the other great books from Fox Chapel Publishing, or to find a retailer near you,
call toll-free 800-457-9112 or visit us at *www.FoxChapelPublishing.com*.

Printed in China
First printing

American Woodworker

HOW TO MAKE
Outdoor & Garden Furniture

INSTRUCTIONS FOR TABLES, CHAIRS, PLANTERS, TRELLISES & MORE
from the Experts at American Woodworker

Introduction by Randy Johnson
Editor, American Woodworker magazine

FOX CHAPEL
PUBLISHING

Contents

8 Introduction

10 Outdoor Finishes

16 Crisscross Picnic Table

22 Tile-Topped Outdoor Table

28 Café Table

36 Patio Table

Contents *(continued)*

125 Shingled Patio Planter

128 Vine Trellis

132 Planter Bench

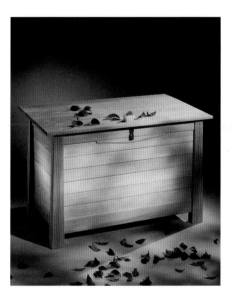

135 Cypress Chest

142 Showcase Victorian Trellis

148 Garden Arbor

Introduction
Outdoor Living

Whether you're a summertime or wintertime woodworker, taking a break from your shop to enjoy some time out-of-doors is always worthwhile. It gives you a chance to shake the dust out of your hair and enjoy some time with your family and friends. Your time outside can be made even more enjoyable when it includes a few projects that you've built yourself. The outdoor projects in this book include designs for yard, patio and garden. Some of them are easy to build with a minimum amount of time and materials, while others provide a chance for you to build your skills and show off your talent as a woodworker. All of the projects will provide added enjoyment to your time spent out-of-doors.

If you're new to woodworking, consider building one of the planters on pages 118-134. They use basic home center materials and simple construction techniques, but the end result will still earn you many compliments. If you're ready for a real challenge and want to tackle a major project, then there's plenty in this book for you as well. My personal favorite is the Crisscross Picnic Table (page 16), but my close seconds include the oak Patio Table (page 36) and the cedar Patio Bar with woven bamboo panels (page 44). Be prepared to stretch yourself if you tackle one of these larger projects, but you can be sure of one thing: all the projects in this book were designed and build by the editors themselves and will provide years of service if properly maintained.

This brings us to the important topic of finishing. Some woods weather nicely without a finish, but most woods, even those naturally resistant to decay, benefit from the addition of some type of finish. That's why we've dedicated an entire chapter (pages 10-15) to finishing and maintaining outdoor wooden projects. In short, you have three options: exterior oil, exterior varnish, and epoxy sealer. Each is progressively more durable, but also more work to apply. Which one you choose will depend on the project and your budget (time and money). I've used all three and found them to perform just as we describe in this book. With all these tools at your disposal, you will soon be building impressive, lasting pieces for your home. You can find additional information on building and finishing outdoor projects at *AmericanWoodworker.com*.

—Randy Johnson, editor

by BRAD HOLDEN AND RANDY JOHNSON

Outdoor Finishes

SIMPLE TO SUPER DURABLE

Outdoor finishes have one thing in common; they all require maintenance. Of course, paint is unequaled at protecting the wood from its two biggest enemies: moisture and ultraviolet (UV) light. Moisture causes the wood to rot, and sunlight bleaches out its natural color. Still, who wants to cover-up beautiful wood with paint? If you want the wood to show through on your outdoor projects, you need a clear finish.

There are three basic clear finishes for outdoor furniture: exterior oil, exterior varnish, and an epoxy sealer with an exterior varnish topcoat. Application ease and service life are the two major differences between these finishes.

Of the three clear exterior finishes, exterior oil is by far the simplest finish to apply. Just flow it on, let it soak in, and wipe off the excess. Unfortunately, oil offers the least amount of protection and it must be reapplied every season. Exterior varnish, on the other hand, is

more difficult to apply: up to 8 coats have to be carefully brushed on. While exterior varnish offers excellent protection from moisture and UV light, it has to be recoated every few years to maintain that protection. An epoxy sealer with an exterior varnish topcoat is the most durable outdoor finish and can last for many, many years. However, the initial application does take longer then exterior varnish.

Garden Sprayer

EDITOR: DAVE MUNKITTRICK • ART DIRECTION: EVANGELINE EKBERG • PHOTOGRAPHY: VERN JOHNSON

sailing ships. All exterior varnishes are formulated to protect against moisture and UV radiation.

Exterior varnish is applied with a natural bristle brush in multiple coats. Manufacturers recommend eight thin coats for maximum protection and a deep lustrous finish. Sand the hardened varnish lightly between each coat.

Exterior varnishes cure to a more flexible film than ordinary varnish. The flexible coat is not as likely to crack from seasonal wood movement caused by humidity extremes in an outdoor environment.

Exterior varnish will usually last 2-3 years before it starts to look chalky. As soon as you see a chalky film start to develop, it's time to freshen the finish. Simply sand the topcoat smooth, and apply a new coat of varnish. Don't put this important maintenance step off too long or cracks will develop in the finish allowing moisture to penetrate and degrade the wood. That will necessitate a complete strip and refinish to restore the furniture. You don't want to go there.

Exterior Oils

An exterior oil finish is definitely the simplest, quickest way to treat an outdoor project. On the downside, it will only give you about a year of protection from the ravages of outdoor life. Oil finishes don't provide a protective film that sits on top of the wood like varnish does. Instead oil soaks into the wood fibers and dries. Exterior oils have added trans-oxide pigments for UV protection and mildewcides to protect against mold and mildew. You'll find colors ranging from dark brown to light amber.

Application is simple: a garden sprayer and a rag are all you need. First, flood the surface of your project with oil. I use an inexpensive hand pump garden sprayer. It's fast, easy and only costs about $8.00. Let the oil soak in according to the manufacturer's directions, then wipe it off. That's it. Done! Depending on local conditions, you'll have to reapply about once per year. The built-in UV protection should keep your wood looking natural for many years (as long as you keep up with the applications).

Exterior Varnish or Urethane

Exterior varnish or urethane (both finishes are technically "varnishes") builds a protective layer over the wood. It offers superior protection and durability over an oil finish. Often, the term "Spar" is found in the name, but this does not indicate any additional or special ingredient. The term "Spar" originates with its use as a coating for the spars on

Natural Bristle Brush

Epoxy with Exterior Varnish

An epoxy sealer with exterior varnish topcoats is the most durable, but also the most labor-intensive finish you can apply to outdoor furniture. This is the finish favored by boat builders so you know it's going to last a long time. Epoxy and exterior varnish enjoy a symbiotic relationship: The epoxy forms an impenetrable moisture barrier that prevents seasonal swelling and shrinking of the wood. This dimensional stability in turn gives longer life to the exterior varnish because it no longer has to stretch and shrink with the wood The exterior varnish returns the favor by providing UV protection, without which the epoxy would rapidly deteriorate.

Apply three thin coats of epoxy. The best way to get thin, even coats is to use a foam roller cut in half. It works kind of like a squeegee. Epoxy cure times vary depending on their formulation and the ambient temperature. Be sure to use an epoxy with a long enough open time (approximately 30 minutes), so it doesn't set up before you're done putting it on. For large projects, mix the epoxy in small batches so you can finish an area before the epoxy sets. Also, for optimal flow out and penetration into the wood fibers, make sure the epoxy you use doesn't contain any thickeners. Always read and follow the instructions that come with your epoxy. If possible, apply the epoxy undercoat prior to assembling the parts. You can recoat without sanding while the previous coat is still soft but not sticky. If the epoxy seems uneven or bumpy, allow it to harden. Then, sand it smooth and apply the next coat.

Before applying the varnish topcoats, I use a card scraper or sanding block with 100–120 grit sandpaper to level the cured epoxy (see photo below left). The sanded surface also provides some tooth for the spar varnish to adhere to.

Rinse the sanded epoxy with clean water and dry with paper towels. The rinse water should not bead on the surface. Beading indicates that contaminants from the epoxy curing process are still on the surface and could interfere with the varnish bond. To remove the contaminants, wipe down with mineral spirits and dry with paper towels or a rag. Follow this with eight coats of exterior varnish, sanding lightly between coats.

Cut up Foam Roller

Sand out any unevenness and defects in the cured epoxy before applying the exterior varnish topcoats.

Oil Finish Virtues and Vices

Exterior oil finishes are a good alternative to exterior varnish. Exterior oils are very easy to apply—just brush or spray them on, let them soak into the wood and then wipe off the excess. Unlike varnish, exterior oils don't form a film on the surface, so there's nothing to crack or peel. Modern exterior oil finishes provide good water repellency. Most offer resistance to ultraviolet light (UV) and mildew.

On the other hand, exterior oil finishes must be reapplied as often, if not more often, than film finishes. This can range from every couple of months to every couple of years. But since exterior oil finishes are so easy to apply, maintaining them is not difficult. Some exterior oil finishes should not be used on outdoor furniture, because they can rub off on clothing. Before you buy, double-check the product's label, or ask your paint dealer to make sure it's appropriate for furniture use.

Finishing your outdoor project with exterior oil has three benefits. First, an exterior oil finish seals the wood so it repels water. Water repellency stabilizes the wood by minimizing the rapid swelling and shrinking that's caused by the periodic absorption of rainwater. Repeated wood movement inevitably leads to checks and cracks—even in rot-resistant woods such as cedar, white oak and teak. Checks and cracks hasten decay by allowing water to penetrate deep into the wood.

Second, most exterior oil finishes contain an additive to prevent mildew (called "mildewcide;" check the label). Mildew causes unfinished outdoor wood to turn blotchy, especially in humid climates or in shaded, wind-protected areas that are slow to dry out. Mildew is mainly a surface problem, but it makes wood look dirty and it will rub off onto clothing.

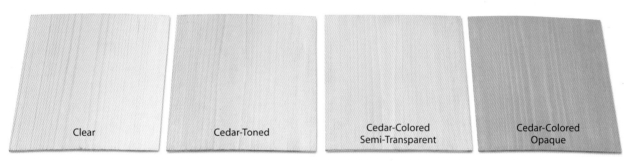

| Clear | Cedar-Toned | Cedar-Colored Semi-Transparent | Cedar-Colored Opaque |

Exterior oil finish formulations include clear, toned, semi-transparent and opaque, depending on how much pigment they contain. Clear finishes (which add an amber color to the wood) need to be reapplied every couple of years, because they afford limited resistance to the sun's ultraviolet light. Opaque finishes last the longest, because they contain the most pigments, but they also obscure most of the grain.

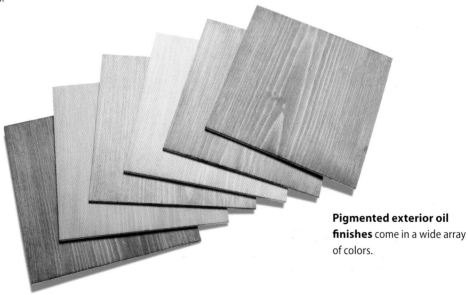

Pigmented exterior oil finishes come in a wide array of colors.

Third, most exterior oil finishes contain additives that keep outdoor wood from turning gray by blocking the sun's ultraviolet light. The sun's ultraviolet light is the culprit that grays wood. UV-blocking additives also protect the finish itself from degradation. Generally, UV resistance increases with the amount of pigment an exterior oil finish contains; in other words, the more opaque the finish, the better its UV resistance. That's why paint is the ultimate in UV protection. Here's a tip: Who says you can't have your cake and eat it too? If you like the gray, weathered look, choose a gray-pigmented oil finish. Then you'll still get the other benefits of having a finish on your outdoor wood.

Show the Grain

You have several choices if you want the wood's grain to show. Exterior oil finishes are available as clear oil or with pigments added. Clear finishes are actually amber-colored, because of the oil they contain—they give the wood a rich, oiled look. Pigmented oil finishes add color to the wood.

Apply exterior oil finish with a brush or spray. Thoroughly saturate the surface and then brush out or rag off any finish that doesn't soak in.

Revitalize Gray Weathered Wood

If your furniture has turned gray or dull, you can restore its natural beauty by using a wood cleaner before you stain. Wood cleaners are often called "deck cleaners." They're available at most paint stores and home centers.

Apply the cleaner with a brush or sprayer and let it soak awhile. Then scrub briskly and hose it off. When the wood is thoroughly dry, it's ready for a fresh coat of finish.

Weathered and gray, this redwood board has gone through many seasons without being finished.

Cleaned and brightened, this section of the board appears much lighter.

Finished with pigmented exterior oil, this section of the board looks virtually brand-new.

They're generally available in three formulations: toned (or transparent), semi-transparent or opaque, depending on the amount of pigment they contain.

As you can probably guess, there's a tradeoff between an exterior oil finish's clarity and its longevity: longevity increases—and clarity decreases—according to the amount of pigment a stain contains.

Soak, Then Wipe

The best way to apply an exterior oil finish is with a brush; you can also use a hand-pump-style sprayer (available at garden stores and home centers for about $15). Saturate the surface with finish and keep it wet until the oil stops being absorbed. This process can take from five minutes to half an hour, depending on the type of wood and the brand of finish. Some brands recommend two or more coats. Pay special attention to the end grain, as it will absorb more finish than face grain. Brush out or rag off any oil that remains on the surface of the wood to avoid sticky, shiny spots.

Maintenance is Mandatory

Knowing when to re-apply an exterior oil finish is the key to keeping outdoor wood looking good. If you wait until the finish breaks down, the wood will turn gray, and cracks, checks and mildew may appear. Fortunately, there's an easy way to tell when it's time to recoat. It's called the splash test. You simply splash some water onto your furniture. If it soaks into the wood, it's time to recoat.

Most clear exterior oil finishes are warranted by the manufacturer to last a couple years. However, a clear oil finish that's constantly exposed to intense sunlight will likely need to be renewed more often. Semi-transparent oil finishes may be warranted up to 5 years; opaque finishes are usually warranted even longer.

Outdoor furniture will accumulate a layer of dirt and grime over time, so hose it down and scrub it a bit prior to recoating. Let the wood dry thoroughly before applying the fresh coat of finish.

An easy test determines the condition of an exterior oil finish. If the water soaks in, it's time to recoat.

User-Friendly Oil Finishes

New "hybrid" exterior oil finishes last longer than traditional linseed or alkyd oil finishes, according to the manufacturers, and allow soap-and-water cleanup to boot. Instead of simply being dissolved in solvent, the penetrating-oil molecules in these finishes are coated with acrylic resins and are carried in a water-based formulation. As a result, these finishes contain fewer volatile organic compounds (VOC) than traditional oil finishes, and their "acrylic-oil" chemistry provides superior longevity.

by CHAD STANTON

Crisscross Picnic Table

IT SEATS UP TO 8, BUT NO ONE HAS TO STRADDLE A LEG

Every summer, my uncle Bob tends the grill at our family gatherings and is the last one to the picnic table. He always gets stuck with a middle seat. We'd cheer him on as he groaned and struggled to get into it—a lot of fun, but not a pretty sight.

Last fall, at our Labor Day feast, I resolved to build a new picnic table with seats that every person could slip right into. I call it the Crisscross, after the shape of its base. This one's for you, Bob.

The Wood

I started designing the table for standard 2x6 lumber, but one day a buddy suggested that I use a new material: thermally modified wood. It's Southern yellow pine that's been heated to a very high temperature, making it rot-resistant. The process also gives the wood a beautiful chocolate color, inside and out, which nicely complements our home's cedar shakes and the artificial stone below it. The boards are amazingly flat and stable. I had to try it!

My friend builds decks for a living. He had a bunch of thermally modified wood left over from a job—enough to build this table. I gladly offered to buy it and had a great time working with it, although I did have to alter my plans a bit. The wood I used is thinner and narrower than standard material. (It's 1-1/4" thick and 5" wide; standard boards are usually 1-3/8" thick and 5-1/4" wide.)

You'll need about 24 pieces of 8' long 2x6s to build this table. The cutting list will work fine if you're using standard lumber, but your top will be nine boards wide, rather than ten. Let's get going!

Build the Cross Stretchers

Begin by making the crisscross stretchers (A). Saw them to length, cutting angles on their ends (Photo 1). Cut dadoes in the middle of each piece using a router or a tablesaw (Fig. B).

Make the pieces that go between the stretchers: the end spacers (B) and middle spacers (C). Using an exterior yellow glue, glue and screw these pieces to two of the stretchers. Sand all the mating surfaces first, so the glue will adhere better. (Note that the middle spacers are aligned with the sides of the dadoes you just

Cut the four crisscross stretchers of the base to the same length. Miter their ends at 22-1/2°. All miter saws have a detent for this commonly used angle.

EDITOR: TOM CASPAR • PHOTOGRAPHY: JASON ZENTNER • ILLUSTRATION: FRANK ROHRBACH

Figure A: Exploded View

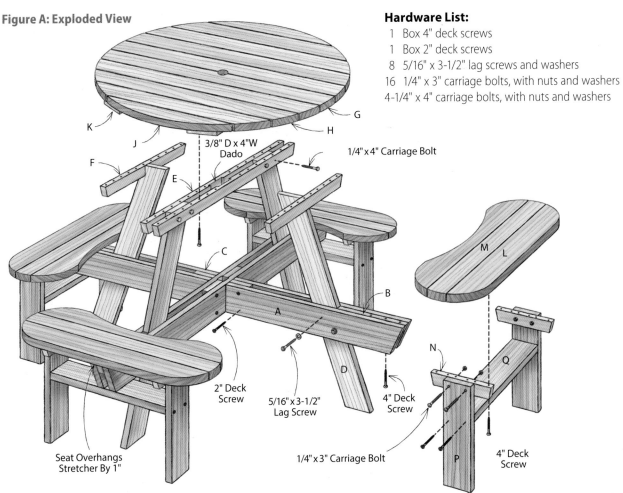

Hardware List:

1 Box 4" deck screws
1 Box 2" deck screws
8 5/16" x 3-1/2" lag screws and washers
16 1/4" x 3" carriage bolts, with nuts and washers
4-1/4" x 4" carriage bolts, with nuts and washers

3/8" D x 4"W Dado

1/4" x 4" Carriage Bolt

2" Deck Screw

5/16"x3-1/2" Lag Screw

4" Deck Screw

1/4" x 3" Carriage Bolt

4" Deck Screw

Seat Overhangs Stretcher By 1"

Figure B: Stretcher Details

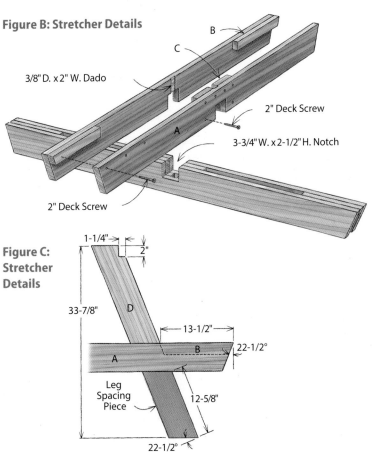

3/8" D. x 2" W. Dado

2" Deck Screw

3-3/4" W. x 2-1/2" H. Notch

2" Deck Screw

Figure C: Stretcher Details

1-1/4"
2"
33-7/8"
13-1/2"
22-1/2°
12-5/8"
22-1/2°

Leg Spacing Piece

Cutting List
Overall Dimensions: 6' 7" Sq. x 31" H; Top is 49" dia.

Part	Name	Qty.	Th x W x L
A	Cross stretcher	4	1-1/4" x 5" x 76-3/4"
B	End spacer	4	1-1/4" x 2" x 13-1/2"
C	Middle spacer	4	1-1/4" x 5" x 4-1/2"
D	Leg	4	1-1/4" x 5" x 33-7/8"
E	Long brace	2	1-1/4" x 2" x 47-1/4"
F	Short brace	2	1-1/4" x 2" x 27"
G	Top board	6 (a)	1-1/4" x 5" x 49-1/2"
H	Top board	2	1-1/4" x 5" x 45"
J	Top board	2	1-1/4" x 5" x 36"
K	Top cleat	2	1-1/4" x 5" x 45-1/4"
L	Outer seat board	8	1-1/4" x 5" x 40"
M	Middle seat board	4	1-1/4" x 3-1/2" x 40"
N	Seat cleat	8	1-1/4" x 2" x 12"
P	Seat leg	8	1-1/4" x 5" x 16-3/4"
Q	Leg stretcher	4	1-1/4" x 5" x 24"

Notes:
a) If you are using 5-1/4" wide material, only 5 boards are needed.

Glue and screw the stretchers together. Note the dadoes in the middle of each stretcher. These cutouts are needed to create a square hole large enough for an umbrella pole.

Cut half-lap notches in the center of each stretcher assembly. It's best to use a crosscut sled, as shown here, to prevent this large piece from wiggling.

Spacing piece

Add two legs to each stretcher assembly. Use spacing pieces to make sure the legs are set at the correct angle and position. Use a long level to make sure the tops of the legs are even.

Handscrew

Fit the stretcher assemblies together. Use handscrews or blocks to hold one assembly upright while you drop the second assembly in place.

cut.) Glue and screw a second stretcher on top of the spacers (Photo 2). You should now have two identical stretcher assemblies.

These assemblies will nest together with large half-lap joints. Draw these joints in the center of each assembly. When you lay out the joints, be sure that one notch will be on the top of the assembly and the other notch on the bottom. The angled ends are your guide as to which side is top and which is bottom. Cut the notches on the tablesaw (Photo 3). You can use a standard blade or a dado blade. (If you use a dado blade, don't take off too much in one bite.)

Make the legs (D, Fig. C). Notch the top of each leg as shown. Round over the bottom ends of the legs with a router. To help assemble the legs, make a pair of spacing pieces that are the same width and length as the portion of the leg that extends below the cross stretchers. You can use offcuts from the legs or pieces of plywood to make these

pieces. Clamp the spacers to the bottom of the legs and insert the legs through the stretcher assembly (Photo 4).

Fine-tune the position of the legs by lining up their ends with a long level or straightedge. Once the legs are aligned, clamp them in place. Run two lag screws through the stretchers and the legs (Fig. A).

Finish the Base

Join the two stretcher assemblies together (Photo 5). For maximum strength, use glue and screws. If you intend to take the table apart for moving or storage (or just to get it out of the shop!), skip the glue and screws.

Make the long braces (E) and short braces (F). Cut dadoes in the center of the long braces (Fig. A). These dadoes are oversized so you don't have to be extremely fussy when positioning the braces. Glue and screw all four braces to the legs (Photo 6).

Add braces to the legs for attaching the top. The long braces have dadoes cut in them to accommodate the umbrella pole.

Assemble the top. Place 8d nails between the boards to create equal gaps. Clamp the boards to keep them from shifting, then fasten cleats across the boards.

Fasten the base to the top. It's easiest to do this on a bench, with the base upside down. Before you begin, though, make sure you can get the table out through your shop's door—it's big!

Rout the top into a circle, using a plunge router mounted on a plywood trammel. First, plunge holes on both sides of each board to prevent splintering (see inset). Then rout the full circle.

Make the seats. Fasten three seat boards together with cleats, like the top. Then nail a plywood template to the top of each seat and rout around the template, using a guide bushing in your router.

Fasten the seats to the base. This operation is much easier if the table is upside down, but you'll definitely need help turning it over!

Add the Top

Cut the top boards (G, H and J) to length. Assemble them in a symmetrical pattern (Fig. D), using 8d nails or 1/8" spacers between the pieces.

Note: If you're using standard-width lumber to build this table, make the top from nine pieces, not ten pieces as shown.

Clamp the top pieces together (Photo 7). Make the top cleats (K) and glue and screw them to the top boards. Remove the clamps and place the base on the top. Fasten the base to the top (Photo 8). Get some help and turn the table over onto the floor.

You can use a jigsaw to cut the top into a circle, but a plunge router equipped with a long 1/2" dia. straight bit will create a smoother surface. To guide the router, make a plywood trammel (Fig. E). Mark the center of the top and nail the loose square piece

Add the legs and a stretcher. Now the seats will support plenty of weight—and even a few rambunctious kids jumping on them.

Rout a hole in the center of the table for an umbrella pole. Make a template with a hole in it to guide your router. Add the umbrella and pour the lemonade!

to the table. Remove the subbase from your router and fasten the router to the trammel. Place the trammel on the square piece nailed to the table.

Set the router to make a plunge cut all the way through the top. To prevent the edges of the boards from splintering as you rout around the circle, make a series of plunge cuts on both sides of each board (Photo 9). Then reset the router to cut one-third of the way through the top and rout a full circle. Reset the router to make deeper cuts and keep routing until you've cut all the way through. Use a 1/8" dia. roundover bit to ease the top's edge.

Add the Seats

Make the seat boards (L and M) and seat cleats (N). Glue and screw the cleats to the boards (Fig. F). Make sure the cleats are parallel to each other—a plywood spacer would help here.

Make a 1/4" plywood template for shaping the seats. Nail the template to a seat assembly (Photo 10). Use a plunge router equipped with a 5/8" o.d. guide bushing and a 1/2" straight bit to rout around the template. Round over the seats' edges.

Fasten the seats to the base (Photo 11). Make the seat legs (P) and fasten them to the cleats. Make the leg stretchers (Q) and fasten them between the legs (Photo 12).

Drill or rout a hole in the tabletop for the umbrella pole (Photo 13). If you use a router, make a template with a 2-1/8" dia. hole and nail it to the top. Use the same guide bushing and bit as you used for the seat.

Figure D: Top Layout

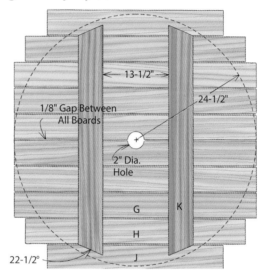

Figure E: Trammel

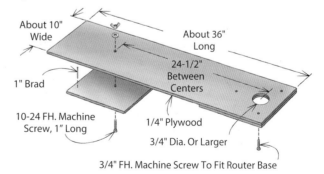

Figure F: Seat Pattern

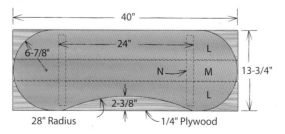

by JOCK AND SUSAN HOLMEN

Tile-Topped Outdoor Table

THIS STURDY WHITE-OAK TABLE WILL LAST A LIFETIME AND WON'T BLOW OVER IN THE WIND

If you love lounging on your deck and need a solid side table to hold your cool drink and snacks, here's the solution. We designed this stylish side table to be simple to build. It's made of white oak and finished with an outdoor stain, so it's sure to handle the weather. The ceramic-tile top provides a durable maintenance-free accent.

Before You Start

Buy your ceramic tile before you build this table, because the actual size of tiles can vary. We purchased a single 12-in.-square x 1/4-in.-thick ceramic tile at our local home center. The actual size was closer to 11-7/8-in. square. The tile is undersize to allow a grout joint in normal applications, but the amount can vary. We used white oak for its natural resistance to rot. Other wood, such as mahogany, teak, cedar, or ipe, will also withstand the elements.

Taper the Legs

Start by sawing the 8/4 lumber for the legs (A) 1/8-in. oversize (Photo 1). Then joint, plane and cut to the final size (see Cutting List).

Next, mark an X at the top of two adjacent sides on each leg. These two marked sides will be tapered. Use these Xs to help you keep track of the tapers. The tapers are subtle and it's possible to confuse them with the untapered outer sides (see "Oops!" page 27). Also, the legs are untapered where they join the aprons (B, Fig. A).

Mark lines for the tapers on each leg and saw the taper on the bandsaw (Photo 2). Stay about 1/16 in. away from your pencil line. After the first taper is cut, reattach scrap with masking tape and cut the second taper. Remove the bandsaw marks with a pass or two over your jointer (Photo 3).

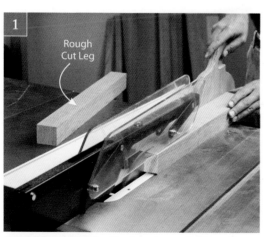

Rip thick lumber for the legs to rough size on the tablesaw. Always use a pushstick when cutting narrow boards. Joint, plane and crosscut the legs to final size.

Bandsaw two tapers on adjacent sides of each leg. Saw each taper about 1/16 in. oversize. The tapers are subtle, so mark an X at the top of each one to help you keep track of which surface is tapered.

Tools:

Tablesaw, bandsaw, plate joiner, planer, jointer.

Materials:

4 bd. ft. of 8/4 (2-in.) white oak, 8 bd. ft. of 5/4 (1-1/4-in.) white oak, No. 20 biscuits, one 12 x 12-in. ceramic tile, exterior wood glue, exterior stain, silicone caulk.

Cutting List
Overall Dimensions: 18" x 18" x 19"

Part	Name	Qty.	Dimensions
A	Leg	4	1-3/4" x 1-3/4" x 19"
B	Apron	4	1" x 3" x 12-3/4"
C	Long frame	2	1" x 3" x (tile length + 6-1/8")
D	Short frame	2	1" x 3" x (tile length + 1/8")
E	Tile supports	2	3/4" x 3" x (tile length + 1/8")
F	Glue block	8	3/4" x 3/4" x 3"
G	Tile	1	1/4" x 12" x 12"

Smooth the tapered sides with your jointer. A freehand bandsaw cut can be fairly uneven, so smoothing might take two passes. Feed the legs top-end first. Use a push block and stick to guide the leg.

Figure A: Exploded View

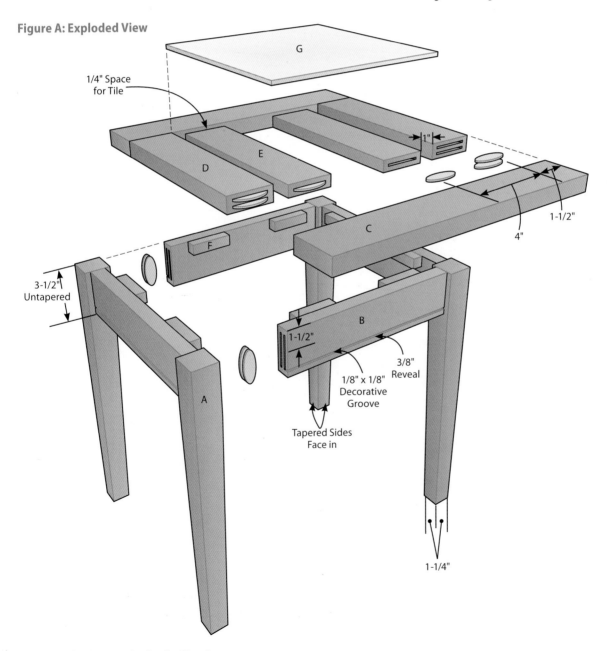

1/4" Space for Tile

G

E

D

C

F

1"

1-1/2"

4"

3-1/2" Untapered

B

1-1/2"

3/8" Reveal

1/8" x 1/8" Decorative Groove

Tapered Sides Face in

A

1-1/4"

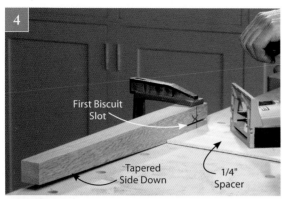

Cut a pair of biscuit slots in the legs. To center the apron on the leg, use a 1/4-in. spacer for the first slot. To avoid a costly mistake, always clamp each leg with a tapered side down. Only cut the slots in faces marked with an X.

Cut the second biscuit slot in the legs. Add a 3/8-in. spacer on top of the 1/4-in. spacer. Spacers are far easier to use than fiddling with the biscuit joiner's fence when you're making these double slots.

Cut biscuit slots in the aprons' ends. Clamp the apron face-side down. That's the side that has a decorative groove cut into it. This time, cut the first slot without the 1/4-in. spacer.

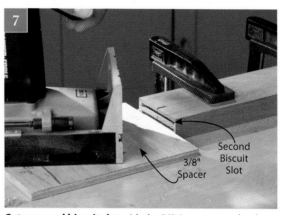

Cut a second biscuit slot with the 3/8-in. spacer under the plate joiner. This is a foolproof system for making the slots in the legs and aprons exactly the same distance apart.

Cutting the Double Biscuit Slots

Using spacers makes easy and accurate work out of cutting the double biscuit slots in the legs. This setup works with any biscuit joiner and the only measuring you need to do is to locate the center of the slot down from the top of the legs (Fig. A). Make sure to cut the biscuit slots in the legs with the adjacent taper down (Photos 4 and 5).

Make the Aprons

Cut the aprons (B) to final size. Cut the decorative groove on the bottom outside face (Fig. A) on your tablesaw using a standard 1/8-in. kerf saw blade. The groove is also a handy way to keep track of the outside face of the aprons during the upcoming biscuit-cutting steps. With the decorative groove facing down, cut the double biscuit slots in the ends of the aprons. Cut the first slot without any spacer and the second one with a 3/8-in. spacer (Photos 6 and 7).

Assemble the Base

First make two leg assemblies by gluing two legs and one apron together, then the other two legs and an apron (Photo 8). Make sure the decorative groove on the apron is facing out. Use an exterior glue for this project. After the glue has dried, complete the table base by adding the other two aprons (Photo 9).

Add the Tabletop

With your chosen tile in hand, use the information in the Cutting List's notes, to determine the correct lengths for the tabletop parts (C, D, and E). Make these parts and mark centerlines for the biscuit slots on their ends (Fig. A).

Cut the double biscuit slots in the outer frame boards (C and D) with their top sides facing up during slot cutting. Cut the bottom slot without using any spacer and the top slot using the 3/8-in. spacer. The tile support boards (E)

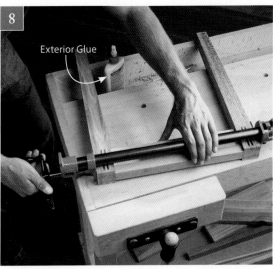

Assemble the table base in stages. Glue together two legs and one apron using exterior glue. Make sure both legs lie flat on your bench. Repeat this step with the other pair of legs and apron.

Assemble the entire table base. Work on a level surface, such as the top of your tablesaw. This will ensure the finished table won't wobble. Working upside down also prevents excess glue from dribbling down the legs.

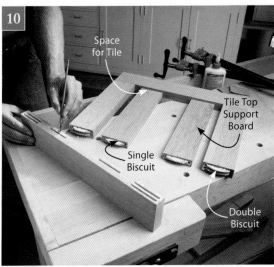

Assemble the top. A small paintbrush works great for applying glue to the biscuits and slots. The tile top of this table rests on support boards that are thinner than the rest of the frame. The tile top's support boards are connected with only a single biscuit.

are thinner and sit 1/4-in. below the surface of the outer top frame boards. This offset provides room for the tile. The support boards are joined to the long tabletop frames (C) with only one biscuit at each end. Cut slots for these biscuits with the supports' top side facing up and without using a spacer.

Next, glue and clamp the top (Photo 10). After the base and top sections have thoroughly dried, give these assemblies a final sanding. Attach them to each other using glue blocks (F). Apply glue to each block and rub it back and forth several times until you feel the glue take hold slightly (Photo 11). Then put pressure on the block for about five seconds before letting go. Leave the table upside down until the glue is dry.

Use an Exterior Stain

We chose to apply exterior stain on our table. Exterior stain is very easy to apply with a brush or a rag (Photo 12). Be sure to work in a well-ventilated area and use the appropriate safety equipment. The exterior stain needs to be renewed every year or two, but it won't peel or crack like varnish.

When the stain is completely dry, glue the ceramic tile in place using silicone caulk (Photo 13). Center the tile so there is a 1/16-in. space between it and the wood frame. This space provides a place for rainwater to drain away. Now you're all set for a lazy afternoon on your deck.

11

Glue Block

Fasten the base to the top with glue blocks. This table doesn't use any metal screws or brackets that can rust out. You don't have to clamp these blocks. Just rub them hard back and forth to squeeze out the glue, and then hold them in place for a few seconds until the glue gets tacky.

12

Exterior Stain

Finish the table with an exterior stain. Let it dry thoroughly before you install the tile top.

13

Silicone Caulk

Install the tile top using four spots of silicone caulk. Make sure the stain is completely dry before you install the tile, or the caulk may not stick to the support boards.

Oops!

We were making such great progress, but we lost track of which side of this leg was tapered and cut a biscuit slot on the wrong side. Rather than make a whole new leg, we decided to repair the mistake. If you make a similar mistake, here's how to fix it. Find a piece of wood that matches the color and grain of the leg you're repairing. Plane the piece of wood to fit the biscuit slot. Trace half the outline of a biscuit, making your outline about 1/16 in. larger than the biscuit's outline. Cut out this "half-biscuit" on your bandsaw or scrollsaw and test its fit. The half-biscuit should fill the slot from end to end and stand a little proud of the leg's surface. Glue the half-biscuit into the slot. When the glue is dry, sand the half-biscuit flush with the leg. If you do a good job of matching grain, the repair should be hardly noticeable—and it sure beats making a whole new leg.

by TOM CASPAR

Café Table

TRANSFORM RUGGED AUSTRALIAN JARRAH INTO A GRACEFUL OUTDOOR TABLE

Picture yourself at a small, round café table with a cup of coffee and a newspaper. The world goes by along a busy boulevard. People are hurrying about their business, but you're an island of calm in a crazy world. Although your backyard may not be quite that busy, you can enjoy the same tranquillity with this outdoor table.

This table is just the right size for one person to spread out the Sunday paper, or for two people to have lunch. It has three feet instead of four, so it sits firmly on an uneven deck or terrace. It has a turned central column instead of legs, so you can comfortably stretch out your legs.

The table is made from jarrah, a weatherproof wood from Australia that's strong and durable. White oak would be a good alternative.

The table consists of four major parts: the top and cleats, made from 6/4 lumber; and the column and base, made from 8/4. Tackle the bottom half first, beginning with the column.

Figure A: Café Table Exploded View

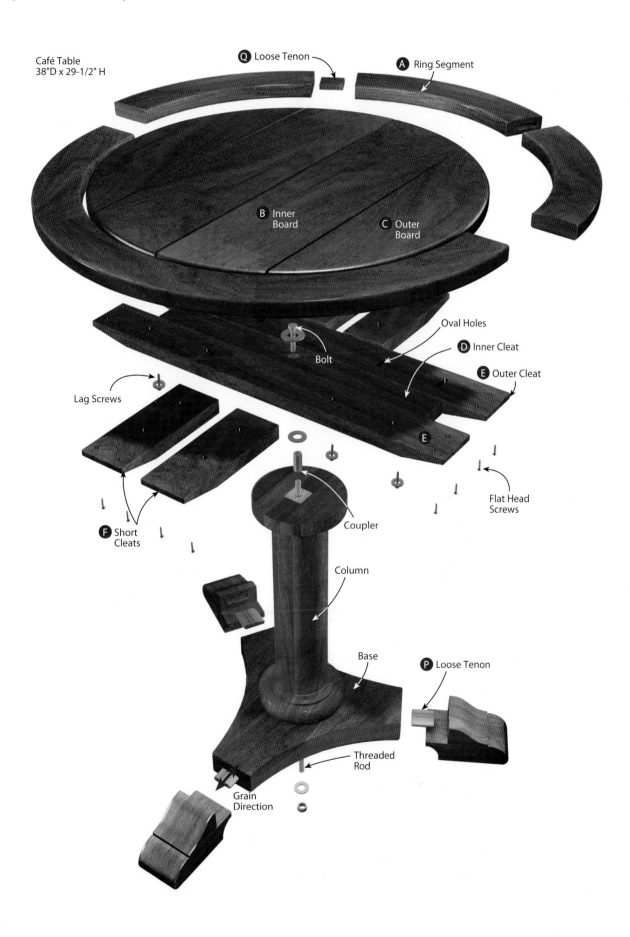

Café Table
38"D x 29-1/2" H

Q Loose Tenon

A Ring Segment

B Inner Board

C Outer Board

Oval Holes

Bolt

D Inner Cleat

E Outer Cleat

Lag Screws

E

F Short Cleats

Coupler

Flat Head Screws

Column

Base

P Loose Tenon

Threaded Rod

Grain Direction

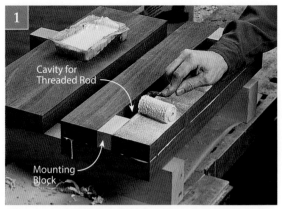

Glue up 8/4 lumber to make the column. A cavity runs down the middle for a threaded rod that holds the table together. Blocks at the ends of the cavity will be used to mount the column on the lathe.

Even up the ends of the column and make them slightly concave with a parting tool. This concave end will always sit tight on the base.

Figure B: The Column Blank

Bandsaw the waste from both sides of the glued-up blank to make it lighter and easier to turn. Then glue on four short pieces to increase the column's diameter at the top and bottom.

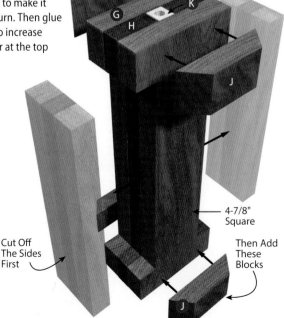

The Column

The column is made from four pieces, with a cavity between them that houses a threaded rod. Cut all four pieces a bit longer than the finished length of the column. Orient the two largest pieces so their heart sides (the sides nearest the center of the tree) face away from each other (Fig. B). This keeps the glue joints tight if the boards cup, since most boards cup away from the heart.

Use a weatherproof glue for all the joints in this table. Spread it on the column pieces with a small paint roller and clamp with moderate pressure (Photo 1). Let it dry overnight. Then take the blank to the bandsaw to slim down the central section before turning (Fig. B).

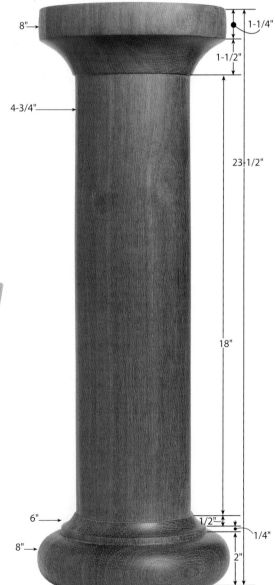

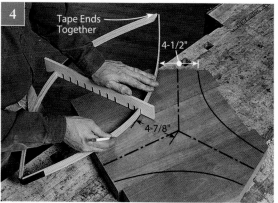

Cut the corners of the base on a tablesaw, using a plywood sled. To set up the cut, place one edge of a plywood square along the layout line and screw the plywood to the base. The saw fence is set to the width of the square.

Caution: Saw guard removed for photo clarity. Use yours!

Follow the curve of a bent bow to finish laying out the base. Make the bow from two strips held together with duct tape. A notched bar creates the arc.

Add four short pieces of wood to the top and bottom of the column to increase its diameter. The growth rings of these pieces should go the same direction as the wood that they're glued to. Cut off the outside corners of the four pieces at 45 degrees before gluing them on. This makes the column easier to turn. After the glue is dry, stand the column up on end and split off the square corners of the large blank to finish making each end an octagon.

Any good lathe can handle this large turning, but the machine must have a sturdy base. Jarrah is heavy! Sandbags on the base's shelf will help dampen vibration. Run your lathe at its lowest speed as you rough out the column. Once you've made a cylinder, use a parting tool to cut down to the diameter of the central shaft in a few places (Photo 2). Then part to the diameter of the narrow ring

that separates the cove and bead. Cut the ends of the column to length with the parting tool as well. Leave a 1-in.-diameter stub while making each end slightly concave (Photo 2). Then complete the turning and sand it on the lathe.

The Base
Cut the base from a glued-up blank. To figure out the least amount of wood you need for the blank, draw a full-size pattern of the base onto a piece of paper. If you make the blank the size suggested here, draw the pattern directly on it, and use the waste for the feet. In any case, here's a way to save yourself some work: trim the end of the center piece straight and square before gluing up the blank. Now you have a finished surface onto which you'll attach one of the feet.

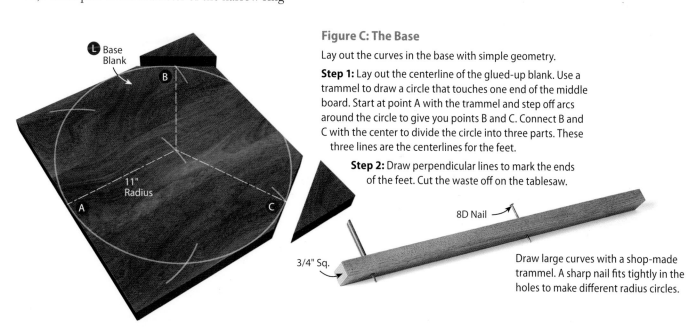

Figure C: The Base

Lay out the curves in the base with simple geometry.

Step 1: Lay out the centerline of the glued-up blank. Use a trammel to draw a circle that touches one end of the middle board. Start at point A with the trammel and step off arcs around the circle to give you points B and C. Connect B and C with the center to divide the circle into three parts. These three lines are the centerlines for the feet.

Step 2: Draw perpendicular lines to mark the ends of the feet. Cut the waste off on the tablesaw.

Draw large curves with a shop-made trammel. A sharp nail fits tightly in the holes to make different radius circles.

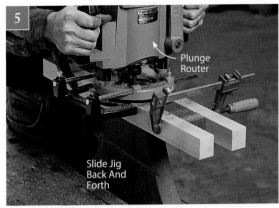

Rout mortises into the ends of the base. Loose tenons will join the feet and base together.

Glue the foot onto the base using a clamping block. The block won't split under pressure if it's made of two pieces: a thin piece of plywood screwed and glued to an ogee-shaped piece of pine.

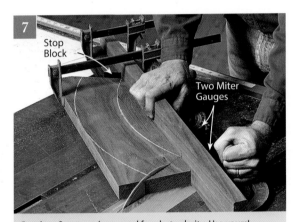

Caution: Saw guard removed for photo clarity. Use yours!

Cut 60-degree miters on six ring-segment blanks. Two miter gauges spanned by a fence make a rigid jig. Each miter gauge was set up with a plastic drafting triangle.

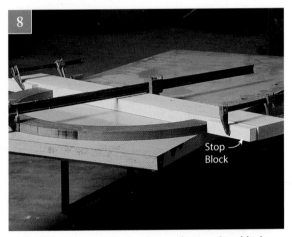

Tighten one bar clamp to glue up the ring. Stop blocks clamped to a stiff board keep the ring from spreading under pressure.

Use a shop-made trammel to lay out the base (Fig. C). You can make a trammel that's accurate enough for this project out of a 2-ft. length of 3/4-in. square stock, a pencil, and a sharpened 8d nail (Fig. C). Drill a hole for the pencil near one end. The pencil must fit snugly. Drill three smaller holes for the nail, to make 9-in., 15-3/8-in., and 19-in. radius circles. Hammer the nail into each hole, as needed.

Draw the corners directly onto the base. Use a tablesaw to cut the blank, using a 24-in. square piece of plywood as a sled to hold the work (Photo 3). Align one edge of the plywood with the layout line for a corner, clamp the plywood in place, and run in three screws to attach the plywood to the base. (The screws go in the middle, so the holes will be covered by the column.) Set the saw's rip fence to the size of the plywood square. Then, cut the blank

exactly on the layout line. Reposition the plywood for the third corner and repeat the process.

Lay out the large concave curves of the base with a bent bow (Photo 4). Cut the curves on a bandsaw and clean them up with a belt sander or half-round file and scraper.

The Feet

Each of the three feet is glued-up from two blocks of 8/4 stock. Cut the mortise for the loose tenon in the upper block with a plunge router (Photo 5). Bandsaw the end of the lower block, sand the curve, and glue the two parts of the foot together. Smooth the sides and cut the ogee curve on the bandsaw. File and sand the ogee.

Radius all the edges of the foot and base with a router, using a 3/16-in. round-over bit. Mill some 12-in. long blanks for the loose tenons. Round their

Figure D: Sliding Router Jig

Steady the router when cutting mortises on a narrow end (Photo 5) with a simple fence. The wood blocks slide back and forth with the router.

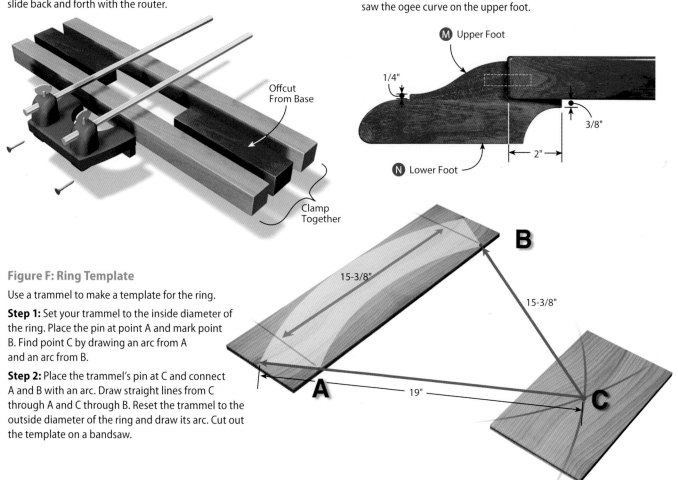

Offcut
From Base

Clamp
Together

Figure E: The Foot

Bandsaw the curves of the lower foot piece first, then glue on the upper piece. Even-up the two pieces and saw the ogee curve on the upper foot.

M Upper Foot

1/4"

3/8"

2"

N Lower Foot

Figure F: Ring Template

Use a trammel to make a template for the ring.

Step 1: Set your trammel to the inside diameter of the ring. Place the pin at point A and mark point B. Find point C by drawing an arc from A and an arc from B.

Step 2: Place the trammel's pin at C and connect A and B with an arc. Draw straight lines from C through A and C through B. Reset the trammel to the outside diameter of the ring and draw its arc. Cut out the template on a bandsaw.

15-3/8"

15-3/8"

B

A

19"

C

sides with a 1/4-in. radius round-over bit to fit the ends of the mortises. Make up a two-piece clamping block for squeezing the feet onto the base (Photo 6). Build the block from pine and plywood.

The Top

All wood expands and contracts with the cycle of the seasons. That's why the top of this outdoor table is made of small units that are independently attached to a supporting framework of cleats. Each unit is free to shrink and swell on its own.

The two halves of the outer ring are laid out, sawn, and glued-up first. Make a plywood pattern of one ring piece (Fig. F). Try the pattern on your rough lumber before deciding where to cut. Mill six blanks.

Miter one end of each ring piece. Mark the other end using the plywood pattern, and line up the mark with the kerf in your fence. Clamp an angled

stop block onto the fence and saw all the opposite ends (Photo 7).

Trace the curves of the pattern onto the mitered pieces. Cut them on a bandsaw. Lay out the pieces in a ring and mark which ends get splines and which don't. (There are no splines between the two halves.) Use a plunge router to make the mortises. Note that the mortises aren't centered side to side. They're offset away from the short grain of the curve. Glue three pieces into a half ring with one bar clamp (Photo 8). Smooth the sides and radius all the edges with a router.

Now you can figure out the dimensions of the top's inner boards. Lay out the top, with spacers, and scribe around the inner edge of the ring with a compass set to 3/16-in. (Photo 9). Cut the boards on the bandsaw, smooth and radius all the edges. Counterbore the underside of the two middle boards for the bolt and washer.

Scribe the gap between the inner boards and the rings with a compass. Spacers keep the gaps uniform during layout. All the parts of the top will be supported by stout cleats.

Figure G: Bolt And Rod Assembly

Connect the cleats with the base of the table with one bolt, a coupler, and a long threaded rod.

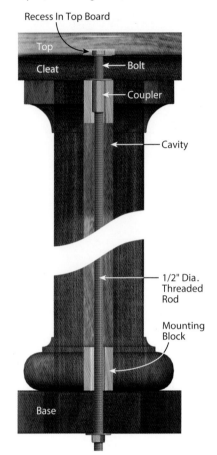

The Cleats and Assembly

Five cleats support the top. One is connected to the column and the others support the middle of the rings. All have tapered ends. Counterbore the bottom of the main cleat to receive the washer. The main cleat is wide enough that allowance must be made for wood movement. Thus, half the holes for the lag screws are oval (see Fig. A). Assemble the tabletop upside down, with spacers, and lay the cleats on top of it. Pre-drill the holes for all the screws that will connect the cleats to the top. Screw down the four short cleats. Drill a 7/8-in. hole in the top of the column for the coupler. Drill 1/2-in. holes in the bottom of the column and base for the threaded rod.

The completed assembly will be very sturdy. Slip the washer and bolt through the main cleat, put another washer on the other side, and tighten down the coupler. Then, screw the cleat to the top boards. Screw the threaded rod into the coupler and slip the column and base over the rod. Rotate the base so the grain of the top runs the same direction as the grain of the base. Add a stiff Grade 8 washer and stainless steel nut, which won't rust. You'll have to turn this nut every few years to re-tighten the table.

Jarrah is such an attractive wood that you might want to put an outdoor oil finish on it to preserve the rich color. The drawback is that you will have to renew the finish every year or so. Left unfinished, the table will weather to a handsome silvery-gray color. After many years of enjoying this durable table, maybe you'll be a silvery-gray, too!

Cutting List

Overall Dimensions: 8" D 29-1/2" H

Part	Qty.	Name	Stock	Thick	Width	Length	Notes
A	6	Ring Segments	6/4	1-1/8"	5-7/8"	20"	3-5/8" Finish Width
B	2	Inner Boards	6/4	1-1/8"	7-9/16"	32"	Rough Width
C	2	Outer Boards	6/4	1-1/8"	8"	28"	Rough Width
Cleats							
D	1	Inner Cleat	6/4	1-1/8"	2"	28"	
E	2	Outer Cleat	6/4	1-1/8"	3"	36"	
F	4	Short Cleats	6/4	1-1/8"	5"	13-1/2"	2 From Column Waste
Column 23-1/2" Finish Length							
G	2	Outer	8/4	1-3/4"	8-1/8"	24" Rough	
H	2	Inner	8/4	1-3/8"	3-3/8"	24"	
J	4	Make-up	8/4	1-5/8"	6-7/8"	3-1/4"	
K	2	Mounting Blocks	8/4	1-3/8"	1-3/8"	3"	
Base							
L	1	Blank	8/4	1-7/8"	19"	16"	
M	3	Upper Feet	8/4	1-5/8"	4"	5"	
N	3	Lower Feet	8/4	1-7/8"	4"	9"	2 From Base Blank
Other							
P	3	Loose Tenons For Feet		1/2"	3"	1-7/8"	
Q	6	Loose Tenons For Top		1/2"	2-1/8"	1-7/8"	
	1	Plywood Square Jig		1/4"	24"	24"	
Hardware							
	1	Threaded Rod	1/2" Dia				25" L
	1	Coupler					
	1	Bolt	1/2" Dia				1-1/2" L
	3	Grade 8 Washers	1/2" ID				
	1	Nut					
	16	Lag Screws/Washers	3/8" Dia				2" L
	16	Flat Head Screws	#12				1-1/2" L

Figure H: The Cleats

Sit on the edge of this table or pick it up by the top. The stout cleats are strong enough to take it.

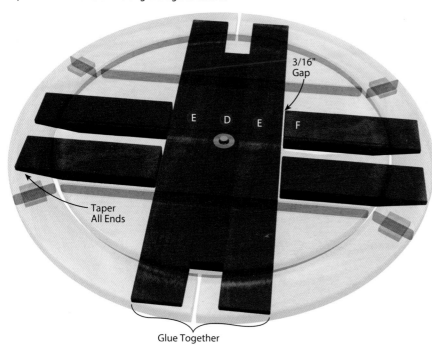

Figure J: Ring Mortise Details

Offset the mortise sideways for strength. The short grain on the inside of the curved ring is weak.

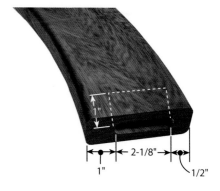

Figure K: Cleat Taper Details

Bandsaw tapered ends on all the cleats and round their edges.

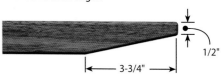

by DAVID RADTKE

Patio Table

WARM, RICH WOOD REPLACES OUTDOOR TABLES MADE OF METAL OR PLASTIC

It's built to stand up to the weather, so it's perfect for a patio, porch or sunroom. The 44-in. top features a stunning sunburst radial design and seats four comfortably. The sturdy base construction makes for a rock-solid table. There's a center hole for an umbrella canopy and plenty of room beneath for the counterweight.

I built my table out of rot-resistant white oak with splines and grooves in the tabletop and dowel joints in the legs. I chose epoxy for strong, weatherproof joints.

I simplified the tabletop's complex construction by using an MDF pattern board that doubles as a machining and clamping jig. The pattern board is used along with a simple trammel to accurately machine the fussy curved joints on the pie shaped slats and to cut the outer ring and the center hub. I'll show you how to make cam clamps that lock the top's parts in position for routing and gluing.

The base may appear challenging to build, but I'll also show you a system, using a pair of ordinary handscrews, to make the job go smoothly.

Make the Pattern Board

The best way to deal with the geometry and joinery of the tabletop is to draw it out on a 4x4-ft. piece of 3/4-in. sheet stock (Fig. B) I call it a pattern board.

Figure A: Exploded View

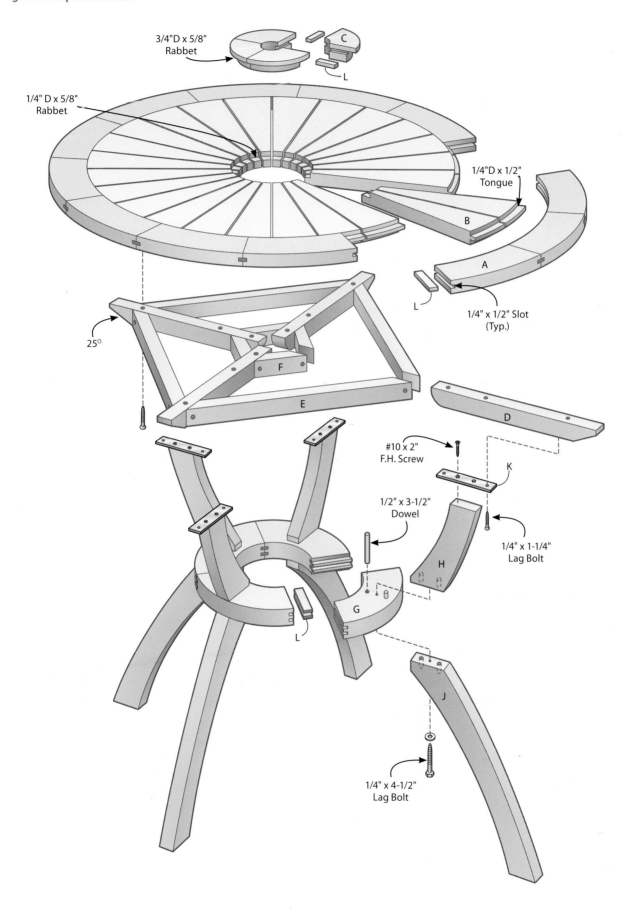

3/4"D x 5/8"
Rabbet

C

L

1/4" D x 5/8"
Rabbet

1/4"D x 1/2"
Tongue

B

A

L

1/4" x 1/2" Slot
(Typ.)

25°

F

E

D

#10 x 2"
F.H. Screw

K

1/2" x 3-1/2"
Dowel

H

1/4" x 1-1/4"
Lag Bolt

G

L

J

1/4" x 4-1/2"
Lag Bolt

EDITOR: DAVE MUNKITTRICK • ART DIRECTION AND PHOTOGRAPHY: VERN JOHNSON • ILLUSTRATION: FRANK ROHRBACH

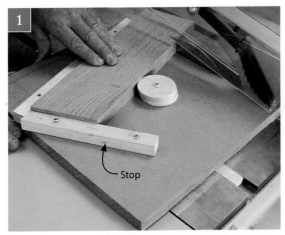

The table is built from the outside in. Start by mitering the outer ring segments with a sled. Cut one end of each segment without the stop in place. Add the stop and miter the opposite end. A shop made cam lock holds the piece in place.

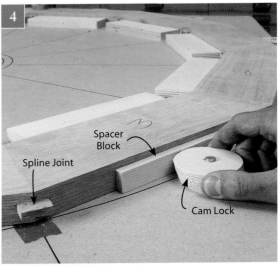

Dry-fit the ring segments on a pattern board that has a full-size drawing of the top. Pin backer blocks behind each segment.

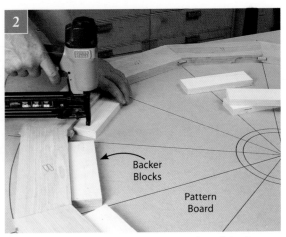

Make eccentric cam locks on the drill press using a 2-1/2-in. hole-saw and a support. The angled edges of the disc act like a cam lock when screwed to a board.

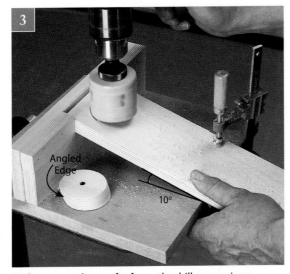

Glue and clamp the outer ring with slow-set epoxy and cam locks. Glue sacrificial spacer blocks to the ring so the cam locks won't get cut by the router in the next step. Tape under the splined joints prevents the ring from adhering to the pattern board.

Build the Outer Ring

1. Measure the length (long point to long point) of a section of the outermost ring on the pattern board. Our measurement came to 11-13/16 in. but check yours since it may vary.
2. Cut the outer ring segments (A) to length on a sled (Photo 1; Fig. C).
3. Dry fit the segments on the pattern board to make sure all the miters are tight. You may have to adjust the angle of the last miter. If you do, mark the joint so it can be reassembled correctly.
4. Add backer blocks to support the inside edge of the outer ring (Photo 2).
5. Cut the cam locks on the drill press using a 2-1/2-in.-dia. hole saw and a table that slopes 10 degrees (Photo 3).
6. Screw the cam locks onto the pattern board so the short radius is just shy of the spacer. The sacrificial spacers keep the cam locks from being cut as the ring is routed out in the following steps.
7. Cut the slots in the mitered ends of each outer ring segment on your router table. Cut splines (L) to fit the grooves from scrap oak.
8. Glue up the outer ring (Photo 4).

Figure B: Pattern Board

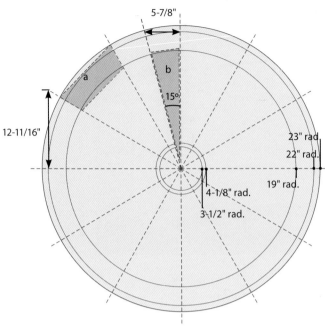

Use a trammel to draw circles with the following radii: 3-1/2-in., 4-1/8-in. This marks the radius of the hub and the depth of the rabbet on the underside. Swing arcs at 19 in. and 22 in. to mark the outer ring. Swing one more mark at 23 in. to establish the long points for your mitered outer ring sections.

Section the whole circle into four equal quadrants (red lines) using a straight edge and a square. Use the square to make a mark 12-11/16-in. up from the 9:00 mark on the 22-in. ring. Make another mark below the line. Repeat at the 12:00 position. Then use a straight edge to draw the blue lines. From the 12:00 position on the 22 in. radius, use a square to measure out 5-7/8 in. and create the black line.

Figure D: Trammel

Drill holes in the trammel from the center of the router bit hole. Dimensions are based on using a 1/4-in. spiral bit for the outer ring and a 3/4-in. straight bit for the tongues and rabbets.

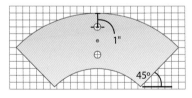
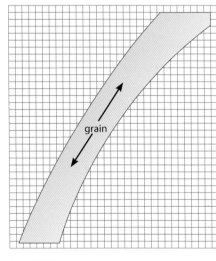

Figure C: Tablesaw Sleds

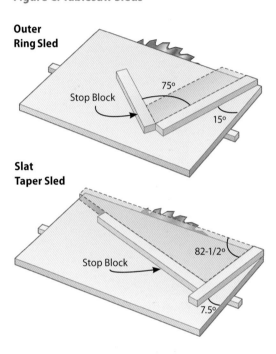
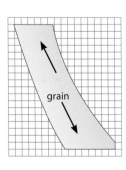

Figure E: Base Parts (1/2-in. grid)

Lower Ring Segment

Center one leg in each section of the base ring and drill through holes for dowels and a screw on the drill press. Countersink the 5/32-in. hole from both sides so a #8 screw will seat flush or slightly below the surface.

Lower Leg

Upper Leg

Plunge-rout the outer ring using a trammel and a 1/4" spiral bit. Make several shallow passes but leave about 1/4-in. at the bottom of the cut or you'll lose the clamping pressure from the cam locks. Swing the router counterclockwise to cut the outer edge and clockwise for the inner edge.

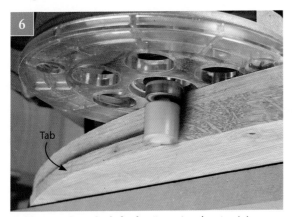

Flush trim the tabs left after jigsawing the remaining waste from the edges of the ring.

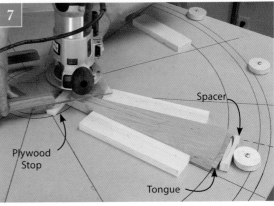

Use the trammel to rout a tongue on the wide end of each slat and a rabbet on each narrow end. Position the slat with the narrow end 3-1/2 in. from the pivot point. Secure the slat with plywood stops, a sacrificial spacer and a cam lock.

Rout the Outer Ring

9. Screw a 1-in. thick pivot block on the center of the pattern board.
10. Chuck a 1/4-in. upcut spiral bit in your router and attach it to the trammel (Fig.D).
11. Set the bit to cut 3/16-in deep. Hook the trammel on the pivot block using the 22-1/8-in. hole.
12. Turn the router on and plunge the bit into the ring. Swing the trammel slowly around (Photo 5). Drop the carriage another 3/16-in. and make a second pass. Repeat until there's about 1/4-in. of material at the bottom of the ring. Important: Don't cut all the way through the ring. You need enough material so the cam clamps can continue to hold the ring in place.

13. Move to the shorter pivot point and cut the inside edge of the ring in the same manner as the outer edge.
14. Remove the ring from the pattern board. Use a jigsaw to remove the remaining stock from the ring. Don't try to flush-cut the edges but leave a slight tab.
15. Remove the tabs with a flush trim bit (Photo 6).
16. Rout a centered groove all the way around the inside edge of the ring.

Make the Tapered Slats

17. Cut the table slats (B) to length.

Rabbet the center hub to fit the rabbeted slats. Clamp a notched, 6-in-wide board to your router table. To cut the rabbet, contact the infeed side of the notch and rotate the hub into the "V". Spin the disc until the rabbet is complete.

Glue the slats into the outer ring. Align the center of every other slat with a joint on the outer ring. Eyeball the gaps between slats. Glue in the center hub and drive a screw through the middle to act as a clamp.

18. Cut the tapered edges on the slats with the slat taper sled (Fig. C).

19. Secure a slat on the pattern board for routing (Photo 7).

20. Set the trammel on the pivot point through the 19-3/8-in. hole.

21. Swing the trammel to make the first cut. Then flip the slat over and make the second cut to complete the tongue. Check the tongue's fit in the ring's groove and make any necessary adjustments. Then rout tongues on all the slats.

22. Shape the tongue with a sander to match the arc of the shoulder.

23. Cut the rabbet for the half lap joint on the narrow end of the slat with the trammel set in the 3-3/4-in. hole. Make sure the slat is face-up for this step.

24. Dry-assemble the slats in the outer ring and measure the exact diameter of the center hub.

Make the Center Hub

25. Cut and miter the four hub sections. Rout slots for splines and epoxy the hub blank together.

26. Draw a circle that matches the hub diameter you measured in Step #24. Cut the circle on the bandsaw and sand smooth.

27. Rabbet the underside of the hub (Photo 8) so the hub nestles into the recess created by the slat rabbets. Don't cut the hole in the center of the hub yet.

Glue the Top Assembly

28. Chamfer all the top edges of the slats, outer ring and hub with a sanding block. The chamfer creates a detail that's visually pleasing while it disguises any areas where a joint may be less than perfect.

29. Mix about 4-oz. of slow set epoxy. Glue the slats to the outer ring first. Be sure to wet both the slot and outer tenon before inserting. Scoop up any squeeze-out that is hard to get at with a Q-tip and then wipe the area with acetone.

30. Coat the rabbets on the slats and the hub with epoxy. Carefully position the hub in the rabbets. Then clamp it in position with a screw (Photo 9).

31. After the epoxy has thoroughly cured add the struts and braces (D, E and F) to the underside of top (Fig. A).

32. Use a hole saw to drill a 2-1/4-in. hole through the center of the hub.

Build the Lower Ring

33. Make a hardboard pattern of a base ring segment (Fig. E). Use the pattern to trace four pieces onto the stock.

34. Cut the miters on a miter saw and bandsaw the curves. Place the four sections together and check the fit.

35. Rout a pair of 1/4-in. slots in each miter. Epoxy the ring together with splines.

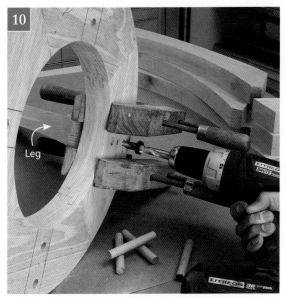

Drill dowel holes into the legs using the holes in the ring as a guide. A screw in the middle hole and a pair of handscrews holds each leg in place. Drill holes in one upper leg and one lower leg at each location.

Drill a shank hole for a lag screw through the small hole in the ring and through the lower leg. The leg is temporarily held in place with dowels and no glue.

36. Once the epoxy has set, sand the inside of the ring with a sanding drum and the outer edge with a belt sander. Label the top and bottom of the ring.

37. Lay out the leg positions on the ring and drill holes for dowels and screws on the drill press (Fig. E).

Assemble the Base

38. Make patterns for the upper and lower legs (Fig. E). Rough-cut the legs with your bandsaw then attach a pattern and rout with a pattern bit.

39. Clamp a pair of handscrews on the lower ring along the leg layout lines. Slip an upper leg snugly between the handscrews. Use an 1/8-in. bit to drill a pilot hole into the upper leg, using the 5/32-in. hole in the ring as a guide.

40. Lock the leg in place with a #8 x 3-in. screw.

41. Drill two 1/2-in.-dia x 1-in.-deep dowel holes into the upper leg (Photo 10).

42. Remove the upper leg but keep the handscrews in place. Insert the lower leg, secure with a screw and drill the dowel holes. Repeat the process for each set of legs.

43. Cut your dowels 1/8-in. shy of the total depth of the hole. Sand a slight flat on one edge to give the excess epoxy an escape route.

44. Dry fit a lower leg on the ring with dowels.

45. Drill a 1/4-in. pilot hole all the way through the ring and the lower leg for the lag bolt (Photo 11).

46. Remove the lower leg and repeat the process for the upper leg using a 3/16-in. bit. Do not drill all the way through.

47. Use a Forstner bit to drill a 3/4-in. dia. counter bore in the lower leg that's deep enough to hide the lag screw head and washer.

48. Mix the epoxy and fasten one pair of lower and upper legs to the ring. Be sure to wet each hole and dowel. Drive a lag screw from the lower leg through the ring and into the upper leg until it draws tight. Repeat for all the legs and let the epoxy fully cure.

Tip If your dowel stock is a little tight, try spinning the dowel in a drill as you sand lightly with 80-grit paper to narrow the diameter.

Attach the top with lag bolts and washers. The lag bolts allow you to easily remove the top for winter storage.

Final Assembly

49. Cut tabletop fastener plates from 1/8-in. thick steel. Prime and paint the fasteners with a rustproof paint like Rusto-leum.

50. Attach the steel brackets (K) to the tops of the upper legs, then flip the leg assembly upside down and drill pilot holes for the lag bolts. Attach the top with lag bolts and washers.

51. Mount the tabletop to the base (Photo 12).

52. Apply your favorite outdoor oil finish and set the table for company!

Part	Name	Qty.	Dimensions ThxWxL	Notes
A	Ring Segment	12	1" x 4" x 11-15/16"	Long Point to Long Point
B	Top Slat	24	1" x 4-3/4" x 15-7/8"	
C	Hub Segment	4	1" x 4-1/2" x 8-1/2"	
D	Strut	4	1-5/8" x 1-5/8" x 18-1/2"	
E	Outer Brace	4	1" x 1-5/8" x 21-7/8"	Long Point to Long Point
F	Inner Brace	4	1" x 1-5/8" x 5"	Long Point to Long Point
G	Lower Ring Segment	4	1-5/8" x 5-1/4" x 12"	See Template
H	Upper Leg	4	1-5/8" x 4" x 11-1/2"	See Template
J	Lower Leg	4	1-5/8" x 4" x 22"	See Template
K	Steel Bracket	4	1/8" x 1-1/2" x 6"	Cut and drill (See drawing)
L	Spline	24	1/4" x 5" x 1"	

Cutting List

Overall dimensions: 29-3/4"H x 44" Diameter

Patio Bar

You'll be the talk of the neighborhood when you show off your bartending skills behind your stylish patio bar. It's got plenty of room for bottles, glasses and bartending supplies. Large casters and fold-up wings make it easy to stash in a corner when you're not entertaining.

This bar is made of cedar and woven bamboo plywood. The 3/16-in. thick plywood consists of five plies of woven bamboo strips. Cedar is easy to work with as long as the boards are suitably dry and flat.

Check the moisture content of the cedar—if the boards were stored outside at the lumberyard and exposed to the weather, they can be excessively wet, even for outdoor furniture (Photo 1). You'll need exterior yellow glue, ten 8-ft. 1x6 boards, three 8-ft. 1x8 boards, one 8-ft. 2x4, and two sheets of bamboo plywood to build the cabinet and top panels, and two 8-ft. 5/4 deck boards to make the mitered frames that comprise the bar's top.

Build the Cabinet

Rip 1x6 boards in half to create blanks for the cabinet frame and web frame stiles and rails (A1–A4, B1–B4 and C1–C2, Fig. A, and Cutting List). Cut each blank to length and joint one edge. Rip the blanks 1/16-in. oversize in width and then joint or plane them to final width. Mill centered grooves in all the stiles and rails for the 3/16-in. thick bamboo panels (A5 and B5). Groove the web frame stiles even though they won't receive panels. Cut tenons to fit the grooves on both ends of all the rails and on both ends of the front center stile. Cut bamboo plywood panels to fit the three cabinet frames. Carefully ease all the edges with a sanding block before installing them; this step is very important, because the bamboo edges splinter easily. It also helps to slide the stiles and rails onto the panels from the end, rather than pressing the panels into the grooves. Dry fit each frame before gluing (Photo 2).

Rabbet all four edges of the cabinet's front frame and the top and bottom edges of the two side frames. Cut dadoes in the side frames for the middle shelf (C3) and center web frame.

Glue up the web frames, middle shelf and bottom shelf (C4). Cut notches in the middle shelf and center web frame to fit around the cabinet's front frame stiles. Cut dadoes in the middle shelf and the center web frame for the drawer divider (C5). Cut the glass racks (H1–H2) using the tablesaw or bandsaw, with the blade tilted 15°. Then screw the glass racks to the top web frame.

Dry fit all the parts to make sure everything fits properly. Then glue and clamp the cabinet sides to the front. Install the web frames and shelves without glue to keep the assembly square. When the glue has dried, glue and clamp the web frames, middle shelf, drawer divider and bottom shelf (Photo 3).

Check the moisture content of your lumber. Anything below 12% is fine. Although this patio bar will reside outdoors, it also contains moving parts and precise joinery, like any fine furniture piece.

Make and assemble the frames for the cabinet's front and sides. These are standard stile-and-rail construction, but the panels are made from woven bamboo plywood.

Figure A: Exploded View

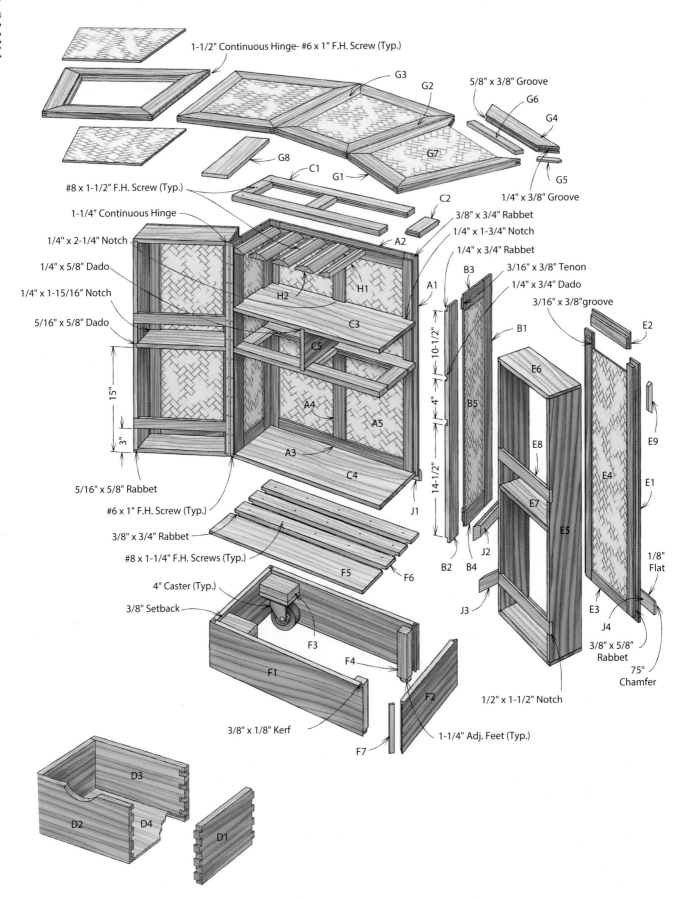

1-1/2" Continuous Hinge- #6 x 1" F.H. Screw (Typ.)

5/8" x 3/8" Groove

G3

G2

G6

G4

G7

G5

1/4" x 3/8" Groove

G8

C1

G1

#8 x 1-1/2" F.H. Screw (Typ.)

C2

3/8" x 3/4" Rabbet

1-1/4" Continuous Hinge

1/4" x 1-3/4" Notch

1/4" x 2-1/4" Notch

A2

1/4" x 3/4" Rabbet

1/4" x 5/8" Dado

A1

B3

3/16" x 3/8" Tenon

1/4" x 1-15/16" Notch

H2

H1

1/4" x 3/4" Dado

5/16" x 5/8" Dado

C3

3/16" x 3/8"groove

B1

E2

C5

10-1/2"

15"

A4

B5

E6

4"

A5

E8

3"

A3

14-1/2"

E7

E5

E4

E9

C4

J1

E1

5/16" x 5/8" Rabbet

B2

J2

B4

E3

#6 x 1" F.H. Screw (Typ.)

1/8"
Flat

3/8" x 3/4" Rabbet

J3

J4

#8 x 1-1/4" F.H. Screws (Typ.)

F5

F6

3/8" x 5/8"
Rabbet

4" Caster (Typ.)

75°
Chamfer

3/8" Setback

F3

F4

1/2" x 1-1/2" Notch

F1

F2

3/8" x 1/8" Kerf

1-1/4" Adj. Feet (Typ.)

F7

D3

D2   D4

D1

Glass Rack

Glue the cabinet together in stages. Add the glass racks, web frames, middle shelf, drawer divider and bottom shelf after gluing the sides to the front.

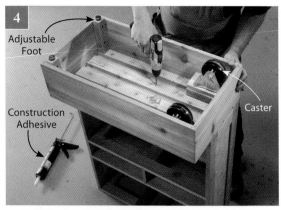

Adjustable Foot

Construction Adhesive

Caster

Attach the base to the cabinet using construction adhesive and exterior screws. Casters and adjustable feet hidden in the base add mobility and aid stability.

Door

Rabbet

Door Box

Glue the assembled door boxes to the doors. The boxes fit rabbets in the door edges.

Protruding Block

Install the doors. Clamp each one to the cabinet, flush at the top, with blocks protruding beyond the inside edges. Press the open hinges against the blocks as you install the screws.

Build and Attach the Base

Use flat 1x8 boards or glued-up blanks to make the base. Using the tablesaw, miter the ends of the front and back (F1) and ends (F2) at 45°. Leave the blade at 45° and cut a 3/8-in. deep kerf into each miter. Set the fence and use the miter gauge to make these cuts. Rip splines (F7) to fit in the kerfs, then glue and clamp the base together.

Cut rabbets on the base top (F5) and nailing strips (F6) and glue them in place.

Glue caster blocks (F3) inside the base to position the casters so they'll protrude about 3/4 in. below the bottom edge. Install the casters. Then install adjustable feet (F4) in the other two corners.

Flip the cabinet upside down to install the base (Photo 4). Apply construction adhesive to the nailing strips and position the base on the cabinet, flush with the front and sides. Fasten the base using 1-1/4-in. exterior screws.

Build the Drawers and Doors

Cut hand grips in the drawer fronts (D2). Use whatever joinery method you're comfortable with to assemble the drawers. Half-blind dovetails provide ample gluing surface and mechanical strength, but half-lap joints reinforced with screws or nails will also work. Use bamboo plywood offcuts for the drawer bottoms (D4). (Note: Dimensions in the cutting list are for half-blind dovetails.)

Follow the methods used for the cabinet frames to cut, assemble and glue together the doors (E1–E4). Cut rabbets around the back of each door. Next, cut the door box sides (E5) and tops and bottoms (E6) to fit the rabbeted doors. Dado the door box sides to accept the shelf (E7) and cut notches for the retainers (E8). Assemble the parts without glue and test the fit before gluing the door boxes together. Finish the job by gluing the door boxes to the doors (Photo 5).

Clamp the doors to the cabinet to mount the hinges (Photo 6). Cut the hinges to length

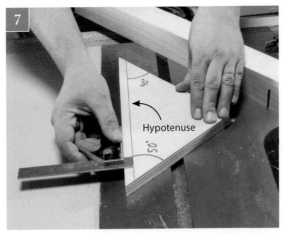

Make two triangles to set up your miter gauge for cutting the top frames. Cut each one oversize. Then measure to make sure the cut is parallel to the hypotenuse. Adjust the miter gauge, if necessary.

Use the set-up triangles to set the fence to cut the mitered top frames. These triangles provide better accuracy than a standard miter gauge. You need two because each frame has four different angles.

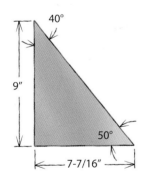

Cut the miters. Use the saw kerf in the fence to accurately position each piece before cutting.

Figure B: Set-up Triangles

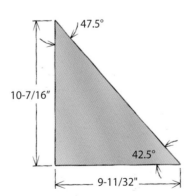

(1/2 in. shorter than the doors) and file down the sharp edges. Stainless steel hinges are best for an outdoor project. Blocks clamped to the doors' inside edges automatically center the hinges from side to side, so when the doors close they'll be flush with the sides of the cabinet.

Make Set-Up Triangles

The bar's top consists of four identical frames that have a different angle at each corner (Fig. C). This presents some challenges, but I had a long talk with Euclid, so there's no need to worry—the head-scratching is already done. All you have to do is measure and cut—accurately.

Make two right triangles to set up the saw to make the miter cuts, one with 40° and 50° angles, and the other with 42.5° and 47.5° angles (Photo 7 and Fig. B). These large triangles will help you set the miter angles more precisely than using the marks on a standard miter gauge—if your saw is equipped with a precision miter gauge, these triangles may not be necessary. When you cut the miters, it's a good idea to use a sled created by attaching two miter gauges to a stout fence. This sled increases accuracy by eliminating play between the miter gauges and the saw's miter slots. It also provides excellent control and stability.

Start with two 12 in. x 12 in. blanks of 3/4-in. plywood; make sure one corner is perfectly square. For the 40°/50° triangle, mark 9 in. from the square corner on one leg and 7-7/16 in. from the corner on the other leg. Connect the marks to form the

True the fit of each frame. Cutting these multiple-angle miters to fit precisely is a tall order, so you'll probably have to adjust one joint. Adjust the same joint on each frame so they remain identical.

Cut grooves in the miters for splines using a shop-made tenoning jig. Fasten a set-up triangle to the jig to hold the workpiece at the correct angle.

triangle's hypotenuse. Measure 10-7/16 in. and 9-11/32 in. from the square corner to create the 42.5°/47.5° triangle.

Cut the two blanks into triangles. With each blank, use a sliding bevel to set the miter gauge to match the angle of the hypotenuse. Then cut the blank 1 in. beyond the hypotenuse. Adjust your miter sled, if necessary, and recut until the cut edge of the triangle is exactly parallel to the hypotenuse. Clearly mark the angles on both triangles, so it's easy to tell them apart.

Make the Top Frames

Start by making a test frame (G1–G4). Set your miter gauge to 50° using the 40°/50°/90° set-up triangle (Photo 8). Then cut the two 50° miters using test stock milled to the same width as your actual stock (Photo 9). Use the same triangle to reset your miter gauge to 40°. Then cut both 40° corners. Use the 42.5°/47.5°/90° triangle to miter the two remaining corners.

Assemble the test frame. If all the joints fit perfectly, you're set. With miters, of course, there's a chance that one of the joints will be slightly off. Don't worry—woodworking is nothing if not humbling.

Assess the situation. You can: 1) adjust your set-up triangles and try again to achieve perfect cuts; or 2) move on, cut the real frame parts and plan to true the fit of the final joint on each frame with your block plane (Photo 10). If you go with the second option, true the same joint on each frame, so all the frames will be exactly the same.

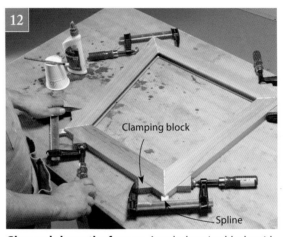

Glue and clamp the frames. Attach clamping blocks with hot-melt glue to apply even pressure across each miter joint.

Figure C: Top Frame Details

by CARROLL DAVIDSON

Patio Chair

CURVED SEAT AND BACK MAKE THIS CHAIR EXTRA-COMFORTABLE

With a set of outdoor chairs like this on your patio or deck, you and your guests can enjoy the open air in comfort and style. This chair is comfortable (the seat contours were patterned after a Mercedes Benz seat!), and so simple to build you can put one together in a weekend. You'll need only basic tools: a tablesaw (or radial-arm saw), bandsaw, drill press, and router.

Because I live on the coast of Florida, I designed my patio chair to stand up to the ravages of salt-laden air, hot sun, and heavy rain. And I didn't want a patio full of chairs that required heavy maintenance. You can enjoy these without worrying about scraping and painting every year.

One of the tricks to building a low-maintenance chair is to select the right wood. I made these chairs from vertical-grain cypress. The grain pattern is visually appealing, and cypress holds up extremely well outdoors, without any finish. Other suitable woods are teak, mahogany and cedar. Another secret to a long-lasting chair is to select the right hardware. I used square-drive stainless steel screws, which won't rust or stain the wood. Also, be sure to use a weather-resistant glue. I've had good luck

CARROLL DAVIDSON IS AN ENTHUSIASTIC HOME WOOD-WORKER. HE LIVES SOUTH OF MIAMI, FLORIDA WITH HIS WIFE, HELEN.

with a yellow wood glue; it's easy to work with and holds up well in moist conditions. Alternative glues are resorcinol, epoxy and plastic resin. Finally, to protect the end grain of the legs and to keep them out of any surface water, I added plastic feet.

Cutting the Frame Parts

Begin construction by cutting the legs. They have an L-shape in cross-section, which I made by ripping the center out of 1-1/2 by 2-1/4 in. stock, leaving a 3/4 by 1-1/2 in. recess. You could also glue together two pieces of 1-1/2 by 3/4 in. stock. Once you have the L-shaped stock, cut a 12-degree miter at both ends so the legs are 23 in. long. When

cutting the miters, remember to make two right legs and two left legs!

Next, make the front and back rails, which have a 12-degree beveled top and bottom edge. Starting with 1-3/4 in. stock, bevel-rip the first edge of both pieces at 12 degrees. Next, flip the boards over, reset the saw's fence and bevel-rip the other edge of both boards. The width of the board's face should be 1-1/2 in. Crosscut the two rails to length and keep the offcuts to use later as spacer blocks (Photo 1).

Cut the foot rail to length, then cut the arm and side rails to the rough length shown in the Cutting List. They will be cut to final length during assembly.

Figure A: Patio Chair

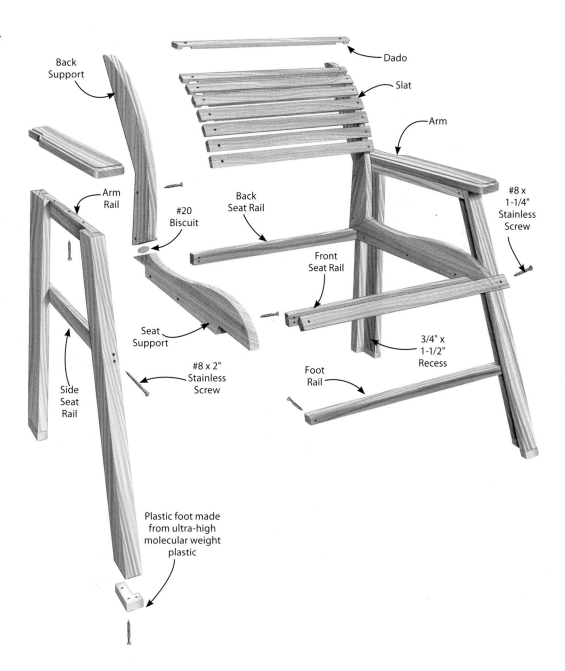

Back Support

Dado

Slat

Arm

Arm Rail

#20 Biscuit

Back Seat Rail

#8 x 1-1/4" Stainless Screw

Seat Support

Front Seat Rail

3/4" x 1-1/2" Recess

#8 x 2" Stainless Screw

Foot Rail

Side Seat Rail

Plastic foot made from ultra-high molecular weight plastic

Assemble the sides on a jig to keep the legs in position. The side rails are cut to fit, using spacer blocks to stand for the front and back rails.

Construct the frame by attaching the front and back rails to the two side assemblies. A couple clamps and a spacer between the back legs will help.

Frame Assembly

I made a jig (Photo 1) to help assemble the sides. The jig has blocks to position the legs so the outside corners are 27-1/2 in. apart at the bottom, and the legs slope inward at 78 degrees. A horizontal block locates the side rail at the correct height (Photo 1).

Place two legs on the jig, and cut one end of an arm rail to 12 degrees. Put the arm rail in position, mark the opposite end, and make the opposing miter cut so the rail fits tightly. Drill and countersink the arm rail, then attach it with glue and 1-1/4 in. screws. To assemble the seat rail, first retrieve the two beveled pieces of scrap that you saved earlier and position them on the jig (Photo 1). These are stand-ins for the front and back rails. Cut one end of a seat rail to 12 degrees, then cut the rail to fit between the legs as you did the arm rail. Remove the spacers.

With the two sides assembled, you're ready to attach the front, back and foot rails. This can be awkward for one person, so get another set of hands, if you can. A piece of scrap cut to the same length as the rails will also help.

On a perfectly flat surface, clamp the two sides, the three rails and the spacer, without glue. If everything fits, glue and screw the rails in position, foot rail first (Photo 2). Be sure to drive the screws that go through the front and back legs and into the ends of the side rails to lock the joint together.

The Seat Supports

The shape of the seat supports is the key to the comfort of the chair. To get a comfortable curve, I traced the seat contour of my neighbor's Mercedes, a seat revered for its relaxed fit. I made a full-size template of the curve from heavy card stock.

To make the blank for the seat support, make a 75-degree cut on the end of a 1 × 4, as shown in Fig. C. There are two ways to do this: Mark out the cut, bandsaw it roughly and then plane to the line; or make a jig to clamp down the stock at a 45-degree angle, then make the cut with a tablesaw, radial-arm saw or miter saw set at 30 degrees. Save the offcut. Attach a 1 × 6 to the 75-degree cut face with a biscuit, using the offcut to help you clamp the joint tight (Photo 3).

When the glue is dry, saw out the shape of the seat support on the bandsaw and smooth it. Glue and screw the seat supports to the side rails, making sure that the bottom edge of each seat support is flush with the side rail. Clamping the seat support to the frame before driving the screws will make the joint tight.

The Armrests

First make a template for the shape of the arm out of card stock (Fig. C). Bandsaw the arms to shape and sand the edges smooth. Rout the decorative cove on the upper edges.

Secure the armrest to the arm rails with glue and screws. The arm should overhang the front leg by 1-1/2 in. (Fig. B). Once again, clamping the joint before screwing will result in a tighter joint.

The Slats

To make the slats, first cut some wide boards to 21-1/2 in. Allow enough material for 23 slats per chair, plus a couple extras. To strengthen the chair, each slat has a dado that fits over the seat support. I cut these dadoes in the wide boards using a radial-arm saw, with a stop block to ensure that each dado is 3/4 in. from the board's end (Photo 5). Once you've cut the dadoes, rip the wide boards into 1-1/2-in. strips and bevel-rip at 12 degrees to a final width of 1-3/8 in. Trim two of the slats to 20 in.—these two fit between the legs and arms.

Drill and countersink two holes in each slat, using a simple jig to keep the holes positioned correctly (Photo 6). Drill holes in the shorter slats without the jig.

Next, install the slats. Start with the three slats in front, including the 20-in. one that goes between the legs. Use glue and screws, predrilling the seat supports for the screws. Then, install a slat at the top of the back, two slats at the "crook" of the seat support, and the short one between the armrests (Photo 7). The upper edge of this slat should line up with the top of the decorative cove cut in the arms. Install the remaining slats, spacing them by eye.

Make the rough blank for the seat support from a 1x4 with a 75-degree cut and a 1x6, joined with a biscuit. An angled wedge allows you to clamp the joint tight. When the glue is dry, bandsaw the seat support to shape.

Screw the seat supports to the seat rail and the rear leg, checking to make sure they are parallel and 1/8 in. in from the back edge of the leg. Shape the armrests, then glue and screw them on.

Figure B: Chair Elevation

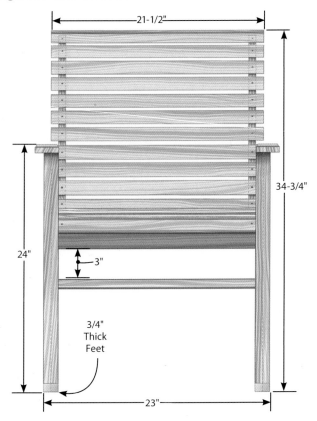

21-1/2"

34-3/4"

24"

3"

3/4"
Thick
Feet

23"

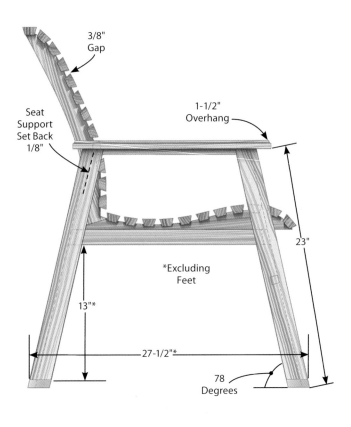

3/8"
Gap

Seat
Support
Set Back
1/8"

1-1/2"
Overhang

23"

*Excluding
Feet

13"*

27-1/2"*

78
Degrees

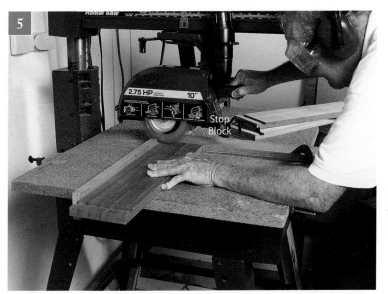

5

Stop
Block

Dado the slats before they're ripped to width, using a stop block to ensure consistent location. Then rip the slats and bevel their edges.

6

Drill and countersink the slats, using a drill press and simple jig to get the holes properly located. Two slats must be cut short and drilled separately. One fits between the legs and one between the arms.

Figure C: Chair Parts

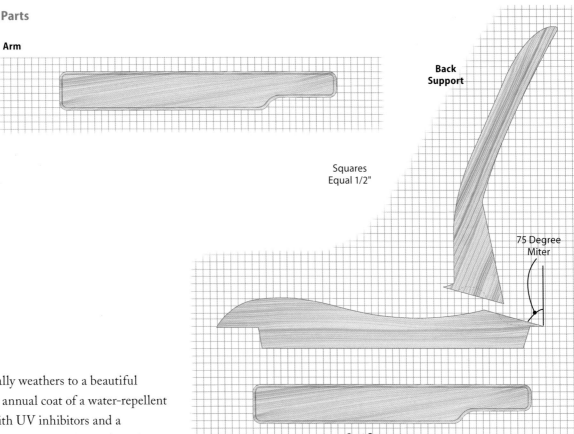

Arm

Back Support

Squares Equal 1/2"

75 Degree Miter

Seat Support

Finishing

Cypress naturally weathers to a beautiful silver gray. An annual coat of a water-repellent preservative with UV inhibitors and a fungicide will keep the wood looking its best.

7

Install the slats beginning with the three in front, then the top of the back, the two in the "crook" of the seat, and the short slat between the arms. Fill in the remaining slats, spacing them by eye.

Cutting List

Parts	Pcs.	Description
Legs	4	1-1/2 x 2-1/4 x 23
Arms	2	3/4 x 2-1/2 x 20
Arm rails	2	3/4 x 3/4 x 17*
Side seat rails	2	3/4 x 1-1/2 x 19-1/2*
Front seat rail	1	3/4 x 1-1/2 x 21-1/2
Back seat rail	1	3/4 x 1-1/2 x 21-1/2
Foot rail	1	3/4 x 3/4 x 21-1/2
Back supports	2	3/4 x 5-1/2 x 20
Seat supports	2	3/4 x 3-1/2 x 23
Slats	21	3/4 x 1-3/8 x 21-1/2
Back slat	1	3/4 x 1-3/8 x 20
Seat slat	1	3/4 x 1-3/8 x 20
Plastic feet	4	3/4 x 1-1/2 x 2-1/2 (bevel to finished length of 2-1/4)

Hardware

2 #20 biscuits

#8 x 1-1/4 stainless-steel screws, as needed

#8 x 2 stainless-steel screws, as needed

*Cut to final length during assembly

design by ANDY RAE

Adirondack Chair

TIMELESS CLASSIC REDONE WITH JOINERY INSTEAD OF NAILS

Visit the Adirondack Mountains and you're likely to come across a familiar style of outdoor furniture named after the region. The Adirondack chair has a low seat, wide arms and a tall, sloping back. It's perfect for reading, visiting with friends or just idling away the hours.

The typical Adirondack is built from pine and protected by a layer or two of paint. Joinery is simple; butt joints and nails do the trick. But yearly painting is necessary to keep the pine from rotting, and joint failure where the arms join the front legs is common. The nails in the arms do not hold well in the end grain of the legs. When you combine that problem with dragging the chair by the arms for passing lawn mowers and the like, it's no wonder this joint is prone to failure.

Our improved Adirondack chair eliminates all these maintenance headaches.

- **No paint or varnish!**
Mahogany never needs finishing and weathers to a beautiful silver-gray color.
- **No loose joints!**
Sliding dovetails and mortise-and-tenon joints keep this chair rock solid through many seasons.
- **No nails or exposed screw heads!**
Plugged stainless steel screws mean you'll never have to get the hammer and nail set out before you can sit in the chair.

The result is a comfortable, low-maintenance chair that lasts.

You'll need about 16 bd. ft. of 4/4 and 12 bd. ft. of 5/4 mahogany. You'll also need a tablesaw, a bandsaw or jigsaw, a plunge router, a drill press and waterproof glue or epoxy.

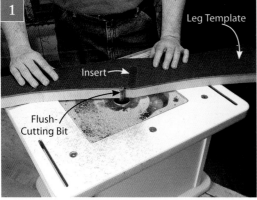

Rout the shape of the legs, arms and back slats using a hardboard template as a guide for the bearing of a flush-cutting bit. Fasten the template to the stock with double-faced tape. Make an insert to fill the gap created by the dovetail sockets in the arm and back leg templates.

Oops!

Oh, no! I forgot to put the insert into the dovetail slot before routing the shape! This made a big gouge in the back leg and I was almost done shaping too!

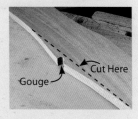

To fix this loused-up leg, I first made a cut parallel to the grain to remove the gouge (see photo). Then I cut a strip from a similar board so the grain ran in the same direction as the grain on the leg. I glued the block in place, sanded it flush and tried it again—this time with the insert.

EDITOR: DAVE MUNKITTRICK • ART DIRECTION: VERN JOHNSON • PHOTOGRAPHY: BILL RAY, ANDY RAE AND MIKE HABERMANN • ILLUSTRATION: FRANK ROHRBACH

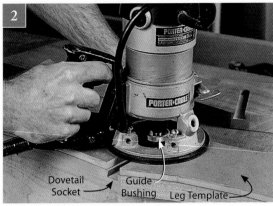

Rout the dovetail sockets in the back legs and arms using a dovetail bit and guide bushing. Set the bit to the depth of the socket, plus the thickness of the template. Then rout the socket by following the notch in the template.

Dovetail Socket
Guide Bushing
Leg Template

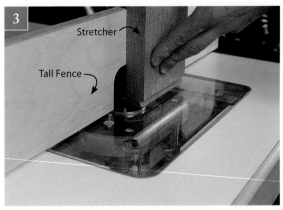

Rout the dovetail in the stretcher with the same dovetail bit you used to cut the slots. A tall fence on the router table helps steady the piece as it's machined.

Stretcher
Tall Fence

Round the ends of the dovetails so they fit the slots in the legs and arms. Make scoring cuts with a handsaw. Then pare to shape with a chisel.

Cut to the Mark

Figure A: Exploded View

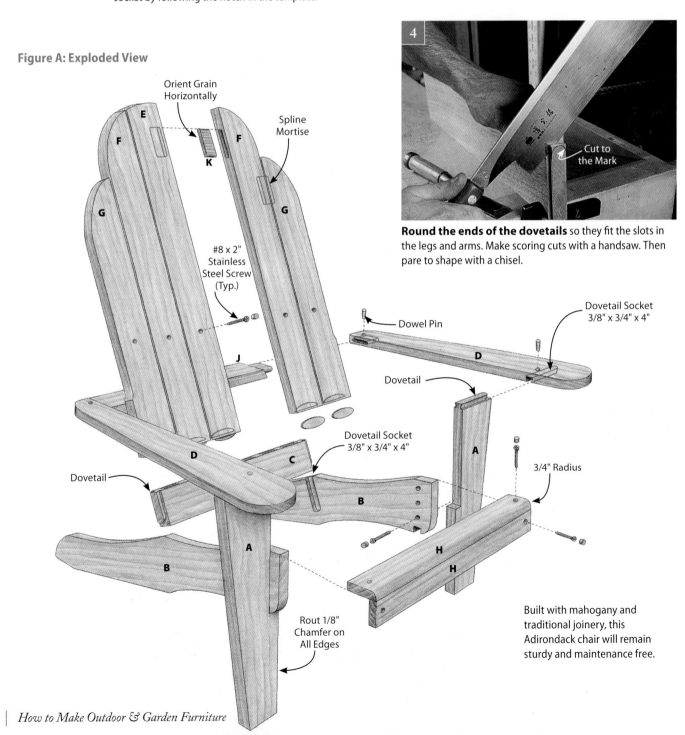

Orient Grain Horizontally

Spline Mortise

#8 x 2" Stainless Steel Screw (Typ.)

Dowel Pin

Dovetail Socket 3/8" x 3/4" x 4"

Dovetail

Dovetail Socket 3/8" x 3/4" x 4"

Dovetail

3/4" Radius

Rout 1/8" Chamfer on All Edges

Built with mahogany and traditional joinery, this Adirondack chair will remain sturdy and maintenance free.

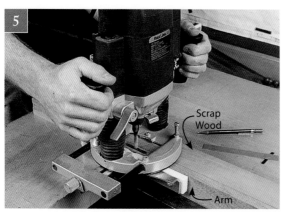

Cut the arm mortise using a plunge router and an edge guide. To steady the router, clamp a scrap board to the bench, and clamp the arm in the bench vise so its edge is flush with the top of the board.

Support the backs of the arms with two sticks. Bandsaw notches in the top and bottom of the sticks to help hold the back of the arms level with the fronts during assembly.

Making the Templates

Template routing allows you to shape a number of curved or irregular-shaped parts quickly and precisely.

Bandsaw your templates from 1/4-in. hardboard to the exact shape of the legs, arms and back slats shown in Figs. B and C. Fair and smooth the edges with a rasp or some sandpaper wrapped around a curved block.

To determine the size of the dovetail notches in the arm and leg templates, measure the difference between the outside diameter of your guide bushing and the diameter of the bit (we used a 5/8-in. guide bushing and a 1/2-in.-dia. dovetail bit). Add this measurement (1/8 in., in our case) to the width and length of the 3/4 in. × 4 in. finished socket (see Arm and Back Leg, Fig. C). Cut the template notches on the bandsaw and clean them up with a rasp.

The Back Slat Templates

Make two templates for the back slats: see Fig. B.

The Back Leg Template

Take the back leg pattern in Fig. B to a copy center and follow the directions for enlargement. In case you don't have access to a copier, we've added a grid diagram so you can lay out a template by hand.

The Front Leg Template

To create the notch on the front leg template (Fig. C), raise the blade on your tablesaw to full height and saw most of the waste. Finish up the cut on the bandsaw. Bandsaw the taper on the front leg. Then clean up the saw marks with a rasp or file.

The Arm Template

Use the illustration in Fig. C as your guide.

Shaping the Parts

Use the template to trace the shape of your workpieces onto the wood. Bandsaw the stock slightly oversize. Now attach the template to the workpiece with small squares of double-faced tape, and rout the work by riding the template against the bearing of a flush-cutting bit (Photo 1). When you've finished routing, pop off the template with a putty knife.

Cutting the Joints

Rout the 3/8-in.-deep dovetail sockets in the arms and back legs (Photo 2).

Cut the dovetails in the stretcher (C) and the front legs on the router table, with the same dovetail bit used to rout the sockets (Photo 3). Round the end of each dovetail (Photo 4).

Rout the back rail (J) tenons in the same manner as the dovetails using a 1-1/4-in.-long straight cutter in place of the dovetail bit. Round the corners of the tenon with a rasp.

Mortise the arms using a plunge router equipped with an edge guide and a 1/4-in. spiral up-cutting bit (Photo 5). Rout slots for the crossgrain splines (K) that join the back slats in the same manner.

Glue the back slats to the stretcher. Use a pipe clamp to hold the back assembly in position and join the slats to the stretcher. Use 1/8-in.-thick scrap spacers to create the correct gap between the slats.

Figure B: Templates for Back Slats

The back slats require two templates: one for the center slat (E) and another for the tall and short slats (F and G). Start with a single 8-3/8 in. x 26 in. piece of template stock. Draw a 6-in. radius at the top with a compass. Rip the 4-in. center slat template from the right side. Rip the outside slat template to 4 in., but stop about 6 in. from the bottom. Finish the 1/4-in. jog on the bandsaw. Bandsaw the top curves and rasp smooth.

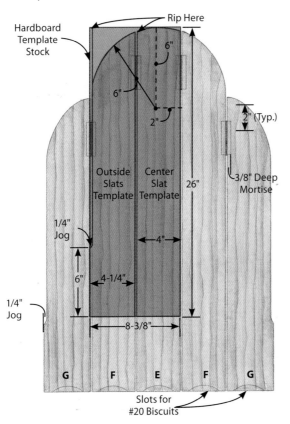

Make the splines (K) by rounding the edges of a 1/4 in. x 3 in. × 12 in. board with a rasp so they fit the mortises in the back slats. Cut four 7/8-in. splines on the tablesaw.

Use a biscuit joiner to cut the slots in the bottom of the back slats and the stretcher. You could also groove the parts on the tablesaw and join the back slats to the stretcher with a 1/4-in.-thick spline.

Assembling the Chair

For the ultimate in weather resistance we used epoxy to glue up the chair. Other waterproof glues will also work fine.

The chair goes together in stages. First, join the back legs to the stretcher. Then, join the arms to the front legs. Add the back rail to the arm/front leg assembly. Use scrap sticks to support the arms while you screw the back legs to the front legs (Photo 6). Pull the arms tight to the back rail with a pipe clamp. Drill and peg the four arm joints.

With the back rail in position, hold a back slat against the rail and mark it for the counterbored screw hole.

Epoxy the splines into the back slats using 1/8-in.-thick scrap spacers to create the correct gap between the slats. (Go easy with the epoxy. Squeeze-out between the slats is hard to remove.) Clamp the back slats together with a single pipe clamp. Epoxy the biscuits in the stretcher. Then set the entire back slat assembly onto the stretcher (Photo 7). Once the slats are positioned in the stretcher, screw them to the back rail.

Installing the seat slats is simple: drill and counterbore all the holes in the slats, then position them using 1/8-in. spacers as before, and drive the screws home.

Finally, cut the plugs for the screw holes on the drill press with a plug cutter. To visually blend in the plugs, orient the face grain of the plugs with the grain of the chair and pare them flush to the surface with a chisel.

Finishing and Care

Mahogany weathers to a beautiful silver/gray patina so there's no need to finish this Adirondack chair. To prevent end grain checks where the chair will come in contact with the ground, apply thinned epoxy.

Figure C: Chair Parts

How to Enlarge this Pattern

Use a copier to enlarge the back leg pattern at right by 200 percent. Enlarge it again by 200 percent, then enlarge this copy by 183 percent for a full-size template. You may have to tweak the last enlargement to get an exact copy. Cut out the outline with scissors and trace it onto a 1/4-in. hardboard template blank.

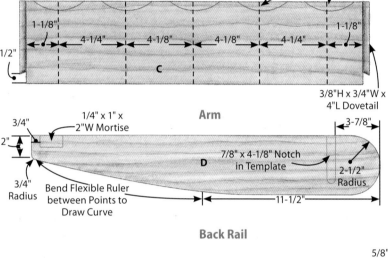

Back Leg

1 Square = 1/2"

7/8" x 4-1/8" Notch in Template

3/4"

37-1/2" B

58-1/2 Degrees

1" 1-1/4"

34-5/8"

Front Leg

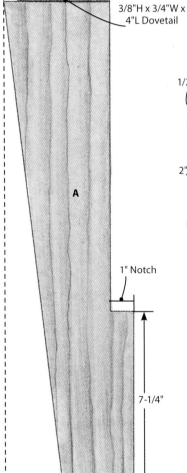

4-1/2"

3/8"H x 3/4"W x 4"L Dovetail

A

1" Notch

7-1/4"

3"

5-1/2"

Stretcher

Slots for #20 Biscuits

1-1/8"   4-1/4"   4-1/8"   4-1/8"   4-1/4"   1-1/8"

1/2"

C

3/8"H x 3/4"W x 4"L Dovetail

Arm

3/4"

1/4" x 1" x 2"W Mortise

2"

3-7/8"

7/8" x 4-1/8" Notch in Template

D

2-1/2" Radius

3/4" Radius

Bend Flexible Ruler between Points to Draw Curve

11-1/2"

Back Rail

5/8"

J

Bevel Edge 58-1/2 Deg.

1/4" x 1" x 2"W Tenon

Thinning the epoxy 50 percent with acetone allows the mixture to soak more deeply into the pores.

This Adirondack will provide you with years and years of outdoor lounging pleasure without ever having to lift a finger, except to move the chair to follow the shade over the course of a lazy afternoon.

Cutting List

Part	Name	Qty.	Dimensions
5/4 Mahogany			
A	Front Leg	2	1" x 5-1/2" x 20-3/8"
B	Back Leg	2	1" x 7" x 37-1/2"
C	Stretcher	1	1" x 4-1/2" x 19-3/4"
4/4 Mahogany			
D	Arms	2	3/4" x 5" x 30-3/8"
E	Center Back Slat	1	3/4" x 4" x 32"
F	Tall Back Slats	2	3/4" x 4" x 32"
G	Short Back Slats	2	3/4" x 4-1/4" x 26"
H	Seat Slats	8	3/4" x 3" x 21"
J	Back Rail	1	3/4" x 3-3/8" x 23"
K	Splines	4	1/4" x 3" x 7/8"

by TOM CASPAR

Adirondack Love Seat

IT'S JUST AS COMFORTABLE AS IT LOOKS

Adirondack chairs represent all that's best about American design: they're practical, with no unnecessary parts; they're accessible, because just about anyone who can cut wood can make one; and they're perfectly suited to their setting, the great outdoors.

An Adirondack's low seat and broad arms invite you to slow down and take it easy. Most Adirondacks are single chairs, of course. A two-seater is something special. Sharing the Adirondack experience with a friend makes it all the better.

Begin building the love seat by sawing out the back legs from a western red cedar 2x6. You'll get the most accurate cuts by using a bandsaw, but you could use a jigsaw, instead.

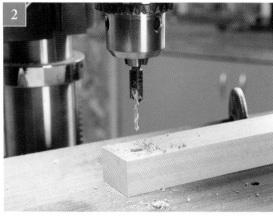

Joinery is simple: just screws and glue. You'll cover every screw hole with a plug later on. As you build the love seat, drill holes for the plugs and screws simultaneously with a combination bit.

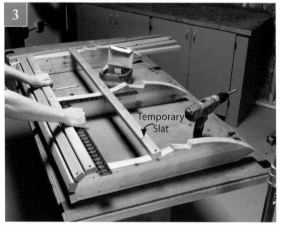

Assemble the seat. Fasten the first four seat slats, which are made from 5/4 cedar boards. Check for square as you go. Temporarily add a slat to space the legs the correct distance.

Temporary Slat

Screw and glue together the front legs. Use a water-resistant glue to assemble all the parts of the project.

Materials and Tools

This project is built from western red cedar construction lumber, which is commonly available at home centers and lumberyards. You'll need two 2 × 6 boards, 8 ft. long, and nine pieces of 5/4 lumber, 1 in. thick, 5-1/2 in. wide, and 12 ft. long. Dust from cutting western red cedar can be irritating, so wear an appropriate dust mask and work in a well-ventilated shop or outdoors. Use rust-resistant deck screws to assemble the project. You'll need about 100 1-1/2-in. screws and 50 1-1/4-in. screws. You'll also need two inside-corner braces and 100 screw-hole plugs.

You'll use a tablesaw, bandsaw (or jigsaw), router table, 3/8-in. roundover bit, 30-degree chamfer bit, cordless drill and a file for the project. A miter saw is also handy.

Make the Legs and Seat

1. The love seat sits on three back legs: two on the sides (A1, Fig. A) and one in the center (A2). They're virtually identical, except for one important detail: the notch for the lower back rail (A5) is positioned farther back on the center leg than on the outer legs (Fig. H). To ensure that all the legs come out the same, make one paper pattern based on the measurements given for the outer back leg (A1). Trace around the pattern on three leg blanks cut to the same length, omitting the notches. Then draw the notches directly on the legs. In addition, set your miter saw to 18 degrees and cut a miter on a scrap piece of 1 × 6. Use this piece to draw the angled lines that indicate the location of the front legs. Draw these lines on both sides of each outer leg.

Fasten the middle slats next. Then install two slats between the middle and outer slats. Adjust these slats up or down to make the spacing even.

Draw a curve across the back using a shop-made trammel. That's just a stick with a nail at one end and a pencil stuck in a hole on the other end. Remove the slats and cut the curve on each piece.

Fit the Back Slats

14. Make a set of back slats (D1 and D2). You can rough-cut two slats from one 5-1/2-in.-wide 5/4 board using a bandsaw. Build a tapering jig and cut each slat using the tablesaw (Photo 9 and Fig. K). The exact angles on the slat's ends are not important.

15. Drill screw-and-plug holes in the lower ends of the outer slats (D1). Mark the positions of these slats on the lower back rail (Fig. B). Clamp the slats in position (the top ends of the centermost slats touch each other) and mark locations for the screws that will go into the upper back rail. Remove the slats, drill the screw-and-plug holes, then attach—but don't glue—the slats in place (Photo 10).

16. Install one of the inner back slats (D2) midway between the outer back slats. It should be vertical. Fit the remaining slats (Photo 11). Make the gap between them about 1/4-in. After these slats are fitted, mark their screw-and-plug holes and cut off any excess length at the bottom. Then install the slats with screws, but don't use glue. Repeat this process on the other side of the back.

17. Make a trammel and find the center point of each half of the back (Fig. L). Turn the trammel around and draw each curve (Photo 12).

18. Mark the position of all slats and remove them. Bandsaw their top ends and round over all their edges. Glue and screw the slats back in place. Cut a piece of paper to fit the gap between the two back sections. Fold the paper in half and use it as a pattern to make two pieces (D3) to fill the gap. Install these pieces.

Support the Arms

19. Connect the arms and legs with inside corner braces (Fig. A). Use #10 or #12 pan head screws to install them.

20. Cut two corbel blanks (B3). Rout stopped grooves on the inside edge of each blank to accommodate the corner brace and screw heads (Photo 13). Saw the corbel's shape (Fig. N) and round over its outside edges. Make sure each corbel's top fits tight under the arm. Drill screw-and-plug holes through the front legs and screw and glue the corbels to the front legs (Photo 14).

Rout grooves on the ends and inner edges of the corbels, the wing-shaped pieces that support the love seat's broad arms. These grooves hide metal braces under the arms.

Fasten the corbels to the legs with glue and screws. The brace allows you to safely lift the love seat by its arms.

Finishing Steps

21. Install the back seat slats. Glue plugs in all the screw holes. Cut and sand them flush.
22. Apply two coats of exterior oil finish. It's best to do this outside, for good ventilation. Sit and enjoy!

Once every part is in place, glue plugs in each screw hole. Cut the excess with a flush-cutting saw.

Figure A: Exploded View

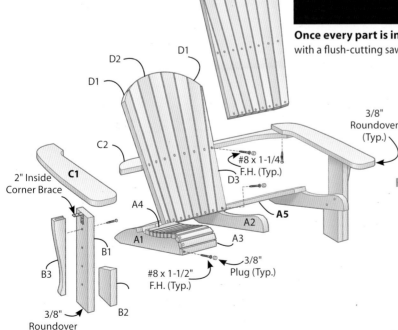

Figure B: Slat Location

Figure C: Arm and Back Rail Assembly

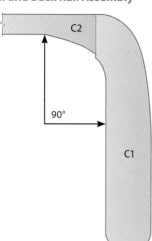

C2

90°

C1

Figure D: Cross Section

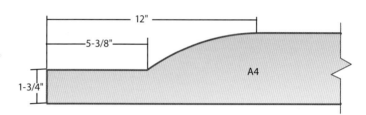

60°

6-3/4"

8-7/16"

18°

A2

13-1/4"

18°

Figure E: Front Leg

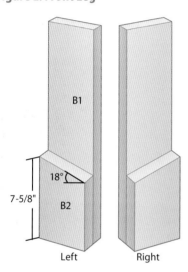

B1

18°

7-5/8"

B2

Left   Right

Figure F: Back Seat Slat

12"

5-3/8"

A4

1-3/4"

Figure G: Lower Back Rail

9"

1-3/4"

A5

Straight
Cuts

3"

2"

2-3/4"

3-1/4"

2-3/4"

3-7/8"

6"

8-1/4"

Figure H: Back Legs

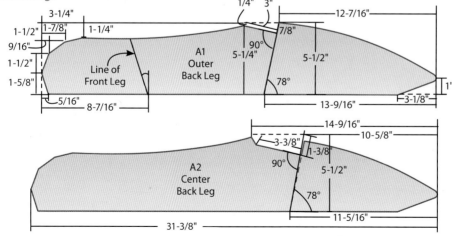

3-1/4"

1-1/2"   1-7/8"   1-1/4"

9/16"

1-1/2"

1-5/8"

Line of
Front Leg

5/16"

8-7/16"

1/4"   3"

7/8"

90°

A1
Outer
Back Leg

5-1/4"

78°

5-1/2"

12-7/16"

13-9/16"

1"

3-1/8"

14-9/16"

10-5/8"

3-3/8"

1-3/8"

90°

A2
Center
Back Leg

5-1/2"

78°

11-5/16"

31-3/8"

Figure J: Arm

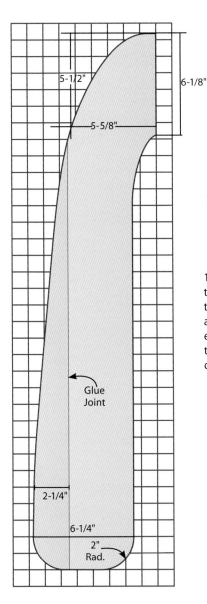

5-1/2"
6-1/8"
5-5/8"
Glue Joint
2-1/4"
6-1/4"
2" Rad.

Figure K: Back Slats and Tapering Sled

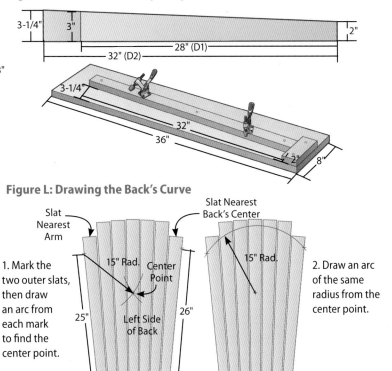

3-1/4" 3" 2"
28" (D1)
32" (D2)
3-1/4"
32"
36"
2"
8"

Figure L: Drawing the Back's Curve

Slat Nearest Arm
Slat Nearest Back's Center

1. Mark the two outer slats, then draw an arc from each mark to find the center point.

15" Rad.
Center Point
25"
Left Side of Back
26"

2. Draw an arc of the same radius from the center point.

15" Rad.

Cutting List

Overall Dimensions: 58" W x 37" D x 34-1/2" H

Part	Name	Qty.	Dimensions	Material
Seat				
A1	Outer back leg	2	1-1/2" x 5-1/2" x 31-3/8"	2 x 6
A2	Center back leg	1	1-1/2" x 5-1/2" x 31-3/8"	2 x 6
A3	Seat slat	10	1" x 1-1/2" x 47"	5/4
A4	Back seat slat	1	1" x 3-3/4" x 47"	5/4
A5	Lower back rail	1	1" x 5-1/2" x 47"	5/4
Front legs				
B1	Outer leg	2	1-1/2" x 5" x 19-1/2" (a)	2 x 6
B2	Inner leg	2	1-1/2" x 5" x 7-5/8"	2 x 6
B3	Corbel	2	1" x 2-1/2" x 15"	5/4
Arms				
C1	Arm	2	1" x 8" x 32-3/8" (b)	5/4
C2	Upper back rail	1	1" x 5-1/2" x 53"	5/4
C3	Assembly support	1	1-1/2" x 5-1/2" x 18-1/2"	5/4
Back				
D1	Outer back slat	4	1" x 3" x 28" (c)	5/4
D2	Inner back slat	10	1" x 3-1/4" x 32" (d)	5/4
D3	Center slat	2	1" x 3-1/2" x 25"	5/4

(a) Cut B1 and B2 from 30" long blank.
(b) Glue up from two pieces, 5" and 3" wide.
(c) Cut two pieces from one 5-1/2" x 28" blank.
(d) Cut two pieces from one 5-1/2" x 32" blank.

Figure M: Upper Back Rail

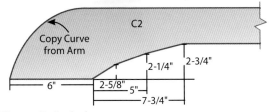

C2
Copy Curve from Arm
2-1/4"
2-3/4"
6"
2-5/8"
5"
7-3/4"

Figure N: Corbel

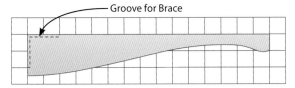

Groove for Brace

by RANDY JOHNSON

Craftsman Style Outdoor Chair

JIGS AND FIXTURES MAKE BUILDING THIS CHAIR A BREEZE, WHETHER IT'S ONE OR A WHOLE YARD FULL

If you're looking for an outdoor chair that's comfortable and stable, and yet light enough to move around, you'll appreciate this Craftsman-style beauty. It's based on a chair design published in the early 1900s in a Stickley design magazine called *The Craftsman* (Fig. A). Originally, I built an exact replica of this chair, but discovered it was too large for the average person and the sling seat was so low and deep that everyone who sat in it responded with "whoa!" and then struggled to get out.

So, I made four additional chairs, changing various parts in an attempt to improve comfort and looks. In the end, I came up with a chair that is smaller and has a stretched-fabric seat. I also added some curves for a softer look. One thing I kept from the original design is the mortise-and-tenon joinery. And for good reason—it's strong.

Tools and Materials

The essential power tools you'll need to build this chair are a tablesaw, a planer, a jointer, a bandsaw, a router and router table, a belt sander and a drill. A mortising machine is not a requirement, but it's really handy for the 24 mortises that each chair requires. You'll also need a variety of hand tools and a sewing machine, if you sew the fabric seat yourself.

It takes about 20 bd. ft. of lumber to build one chair; we used mahogany. A less-expensive option is to use a construction lumber, such as pine 2x4s and 2x6s. If you use construction-grade pine, let it dry for a couple of weeks indoors before using it. If you don't, your parts

are likely to warp and twist. The chair seat requires 2-1/3 yards of fabric. You will also need some galvanized screws and weather-resistant glue.

Make One or Make a Dozen

Because this project lends itself to being mass-produced, we show you how to use jigs and fixtures to produce multiples. However, if you only want to make one or two of these chairs, you can skip one or all of the jigs and fixtures. If you do skip the jigs and fixtures, you'll have to be very careful about measuring and cutting, because without them it's easier to make a mistake.

Figure A
The original Craftsman chair design, circa early 1900s.

Mark the mortise locations on the legs. Pairing up the legs improves the accuracy of the layout. Mortise-and-tenon joinery is a good choice for this outdoor chair because it provides strength and durability.

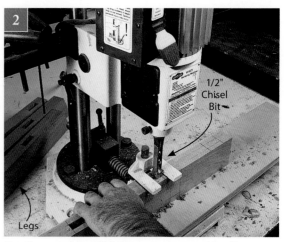

Cut the mortises. With 24 to cut, use a machine if you can, it's much faster! All the mortises in this chair are 13/16-in. deep.

Getting Started

It saves a lot of time if you cut all the parts to rough dimensions and machine them to final thickness and width as a group. There are a couple of exceptions to this. The feet (J and K), the back posts (M) and the armrests (N) get cut to final width later on. Only machine them to final thickness and joint one edge for now. See the Cutting List for dimensions.

Detail 1:
Leg Mortise Layout

All mortises are 1/2-in. wide by 13/16-in. deep, unless noted.

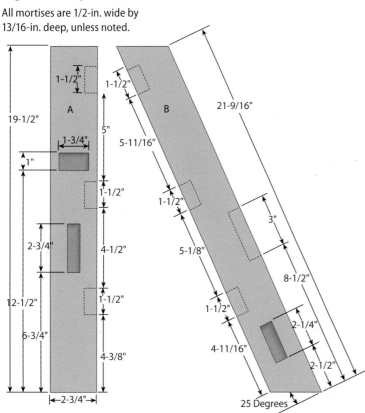

Mortising the Legs

When it comes to mortise-and-tenon joinery, always make the mortises first and fit the tenons second. It's easier to fit a tenon to a mortise than the other way around.

Start by laying out the mortises (Detail 1, at left, and Photo 1) on the legs (A and B). Then make the mortises in the legs with a mortising machine (Photo 2) or drill and hand chisel the mortises or use a plunge router with a template guide. All the mortises are 13/16-in. deep and 1/2-in. wide, except the mortises for the front seat stretcher (Part H, Detail 4, Fig. B), which is 1-in. wide. I find the easiest way to cut this wide mortise is with the help of a spacer along the fence (Photo 3).

Cutting the Rails and Stretchers

These angled rails and tenons can be pretty intimidating, but if you build the cut-off sled (Fig. D) and follow the cutting sequence (Fig. C) they're quite doable.

The main purpose of the cut-off sled (Photo 4) is to cut the side rails (C, D and E) to an accurate length so they will fit the legs without any gaps (see Oops!, page 79).

Now cut the front and back rails (F and G) and stretchers (H and L) to length. Also, cut the miter at the bottom end of the back posts (M) (Detail 3, Fig. B and Fig. F). This saves time later on because you only have to set up your dado blade once to cut all the tenons.

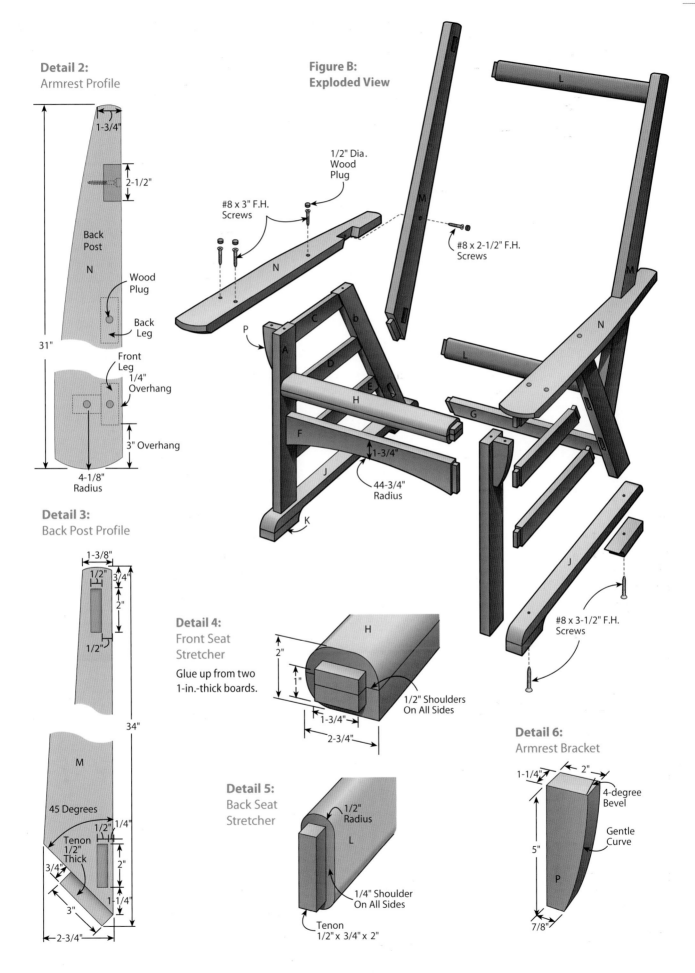

Detail 2:
Armrest Profile

1-3/4"

2-1/2"

Back Post
N

31"

Wood Plug

Back Leg

Front Leg

1/4" Overhang

3" Overhang

4-1/8" Radius

Detail 3:
Back Post Profile

1-3/8"

3/4"

1/2"

2"

1/2"

34"

M

45 Degrees

Tenon 1/2" Thick

3/4"

3"

2-3/4"

1/2"

1/4"

2"

1-1/4"

Figure B:
Exploded View

1/2" Dia. Wood Plug

#8 x 3" F.H. Screws

#8 x 2-1/2" F.H. Screws

M

N

P

A

C

b

D

E

H

F

G

L

L

M

N

J

K

1-3/4"

44-3/4" Radius

J

#8 x 3-1/2" F.H. Screws

Detail 4:
Front Seat Stretcher

Glue up from two 1-in.-thick boards.

H

2"

1"

1-3/4"

2-3/4"

1/2" Shoulders On All Sides

Detail 5:
Back Seat Stretcher

1/2" Radius

L

1/4" Shoulder On All Sides

Tenon 1/2" x 3/4" x 2"

Detail 6:
Armrest Bracket

1-1/4"

2"

4-degree Bevel

Gentle Curve

5"

P

7/8"

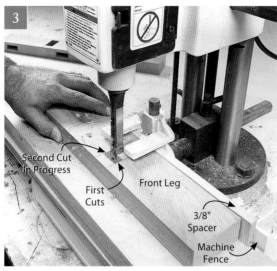

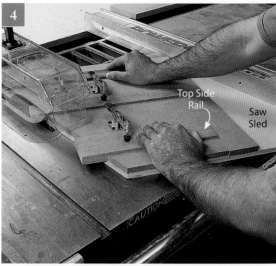

Cut the wide cross-grain mortise for the front seat stretcher in four steps. 1. Cut the first set of holes. 2. Add the spacer and make the second set of holes. 3. Flip the leg end for end. 4. Repeat steps one and two.

Cut the angled ends of all three side rails at once using a cut-off sled. This sled takes the guesswork out of measuring and allows you to make multiple parts with ease.

Figure C:
Side Rail Cutting Sequence

1 Cut the front ends square.

2 Cut mitered ends with cut-off sled (Photo 4 and Fig. D).

3 Cut the tenons to thickness with the dado setup (Photo 5).

4 Cut the straight tenons to width with the dado setup.

5 Cut the mitered tenons and the wide shoulders on the top rail with a bandsaw (Photo 6).

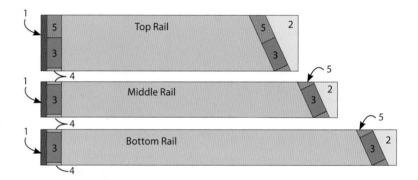

Figure D:
Cut-Off Sled for Side Rails

To build this sled, start with a piece of 3/4-in. plywood cut to 19-1/4-in. wide by 30-in. long. On this piece of plywood, lay out the 25-degree angle that will go against the tablesaw rip fence. Rough cut this angle with your bandsaw or jigsaw. True it up with a router and straightedge. Then, set your tablesaw to 18-1/2 in. and cut the other 25-degree angle. Add the 1/2-in. MDF spacer on top and the toggle clamps and you're ready to go.

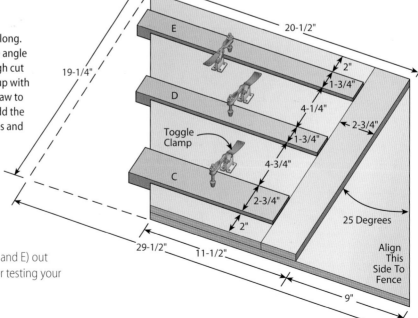

 Tip Cut a couple extra rails (C, D and E) out of scrap wood to use later for testing your tenon-cutting setup.

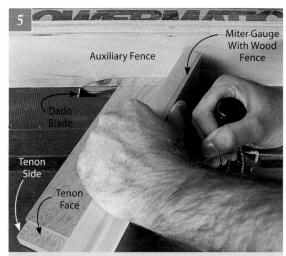

Caution: The blade guard must be removed for this cut. Be careful.

Cut the tenons on the rails and stretchers using a dado blade on your tablesaw. For the angled tenons, set your miter to match the angle and run the end of the tenon against the fence.

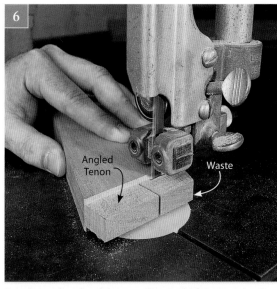

Bandsaw the shoulders on the angled tenons. It takes a careful hand, but it's quick. A fine-tooth handsaw works as well.

Cutting the Tenons

Everyone has their favorite way to cut tenons, and this is mine. (I also think it's the quickest and easiest way to cut angled tenons.)

Start by setting up your dado blade for a 13/16-in.-wide cut. Add an auxiliary wood fence to your tablesaw (Photo 5), and make fence adjustments for a perfect 3/4-in.-wide cut. All the tenons for this chair are 3/4-in. long.

Now set the dado blade for a 1/8-in.-deep cut. Cut a tenon on a test rail and check the fit. When the fit is right, cut all four sides of the straight tenons on the rails (C, D, E, F and G). For the angled tenons on the side rails (C, D and E), adjust your miter gauge to match the angle (Photo 5), and cut the tenon faces with this setup. Readjust the angle on your miter gauge and cut the other side of the angled tenons. Cut the shoulders on the angled tenons with your bandsaw (Photo 6) or with a handsaw.

Raise the dado blade to 1/4-in. for the back seat stretchers (L) and the angled tenons on the back posts (M). Raise it to 1/2-in. for the front seat stretcher (H).

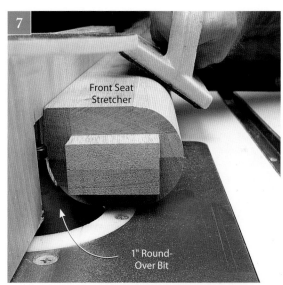

Round over three corners on the front seat stretcher with a 1-in. round-over bit in your router table. These large round-overs can also be made by hand planing. The fourth corner is left square. This provides a larger, flat surface to attach the fabric seat to later.

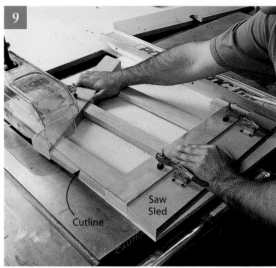

Clamp the leg frames using a notched clamping caul. The notches keep the clamping pressure in line with the rails and provide a flat surface for the clamp jaws to hold onto. The hooked end keeps the caul from sliding under pressure.

Taper the top of the leg frames with a saw sled. If you are only making one or two chairs, you can forgo this sled and just use a bandsaw and belt sander.

Figure E:
Cut-Off Sled for Leg Frames

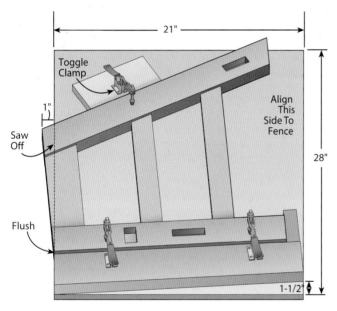

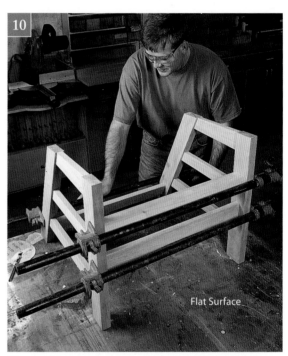

Glue and clamp the chair base. Assemble the base on a flat surface and make sure all the legs are touching the benchtop.

Tip

When assembling the leg frames, it works best to insert the angled tenons into the back leg first and then add the front leg.

Assembling the Base

I scratched my head a bit about the best way to clamp the angled leg frames. I decided to make a notched clamping caul out of a 2x4 and it worked perfectly (Photo 8).

Be sure to test-fit and sand all the parts before final gluing. While you're waiting for the glue to dry, rout the large round-overs on the front seat stretcher with a 1-in. round-over router bit (Part H, Photo 7).

Next, round both sides of the back seat stretchers (Parts L, Detail 5, Fig. B). A 1/2- in. round-over bit in your router table will do the job. Bandsaw the arch in the front rail (Part F, Fig. B) now.

The side leg frames need to be tapered at the top so the armrests will slope. A tablesaw sled makes this process quick and accurate (Fig. E and Photo 9). You can now assemble the entire chair base (Photo 10).

The foot assemblies are made by gluing the foot blocks (K) to the foot rails (J). After the glue is dry, joint and plane this assembly to final width and cut to final length. The curves can now be bandsawn and sanded. Attach the foot assembly with a single screw at each leg (Photo 11).

Loose Joint

Dry-fit the leg frames to check for any loose joints.

Oops!

When building the prototype for this chair, I didn't use the crosscut sled to cut the angled rails. I cut the rails one at a time instead. My measuring wasn't as accurate as I thought! I ended up with a gap at one of the joints (photo at left). I managed a slick fix by trimming off the top of the tenons on that rail (photo below, left and illustration below). This opened up a small gap (photo below) on the lower side of the tenon, but this was easily filled by gluing in a small wedge of wood.

Top of Tenon

Chisel or bandsaw a small amount off the top of both tenons on the loose rails.

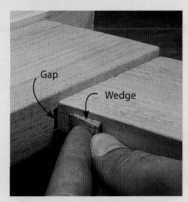

Gap

Wedge

Fill in any gap at the bottom of the tenon with a small wedge.

If an angled joint has a gap, trim the top side of both tenons so you can slide the rail up until the joint is tight.

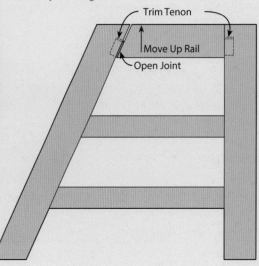

Trim Tenon

Move Up Rail

Open Joint

Attach the foot assembly with one screw at each leg. Drill pilot holes in the feet and legs to lessen the chance of anything cracking. I don't use glue here so the foot assemblies can easily be replaced if they become worn or suffer decay.

Taper the back post with the help of a planer sled. Wax the bottom of the sled so it feeds smoothly through your planer. You can also make this taper with your jointer or a hand plane.

Figure F: Back Post Cutting Sequence

1 Cut the miter at 45 degrees.

2 Cut the tenon to thickness with the dado setup (Photo 5).

3 Cut the tenon to width with a bandsaw (Photo 6).

4 Cut the back post to final length.

5 Rough-cut the taper with a bandsaw.

6 Plane the taper with the planer sled (Photo 12, Fig. G).

7 Cut the mortises 13/16-in. deep.

8 Round over the top end.

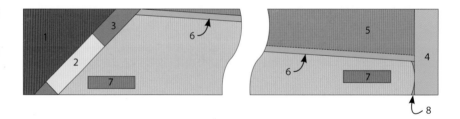

Figure G: Back Post Planer Sled

This sled ensures you an accurate taper on the back post and provides a quick way to make all of your back posts identical, if you are making multiples.

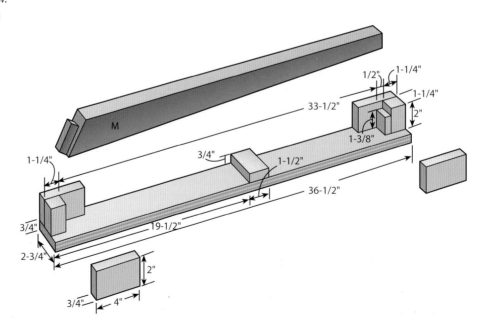

Assemble the back frame with glue and clamps. Check for square by measuring corner to corner.

Attach the back frame to the base with the help of angled clamping blocks and a 2x4. This arrangement puts pressure at a right angle to the joint and keeps everything tight until the glue dries.

Adding the Back

Complete the back posts (Parts M, Detail 3, Fig. B) by following the cutting sequence in Fig. F. The planer sled (Photo 12, Fig. G) takes the guesswork out of getting an accurate angle.

When you're done making the back posts, glue and clamp the back frame together (Photo 13). Clamp the back frame to the base with the help of a couple of angled clamping blocks (Fig. H) and a 2x4 clamping block (Photo 14). The real secret to clamping angles is to keep the clamping pressure at a right angle to the joint.

Fitting the Armrests

To make the armrests, follow the cutting sequence in Fig. J and fit them to the back posts (Photos 16 and 17). Counterbore for the wood plugs and drill pilot holes for the screws (Fig. B). Attach the armrests with glue and screws (Photo 18).

Make the armrest brackets (Detail 6, Fig. B) and glue and clamp them to the front legs. When the glue is dry, add a screw through the armrest from the top. Finally, make the plugs with a plug cutter and plug all the screw holes.

Figure H: Angled Clamping Block

This block makes it possible to easily clamp the angled back frame to the chair base.

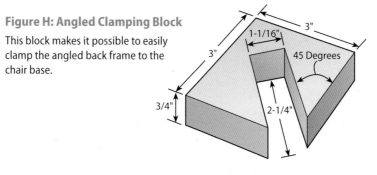

Figure J: Armrest Cutting Sequence

1. Bandsaw and sand the front curve.
2. Rough-cut the side curve with a bandsaw.
3. Trim the armrest to final length.
4. Rout the chamfer on the front edge.
5. Rout the final side curve with the router template (Photo 15, Fig.K).
6. Sand the back end round.
7. Cut the notches for the back posts (Photos 16 and 17).

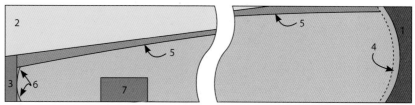

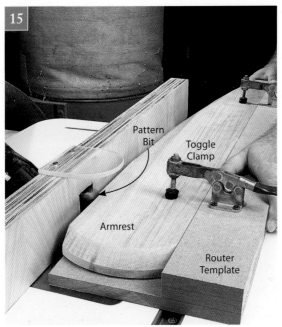

Rout the side profile on the armrest with the router template and a large pattern bit. A belt sander can do the job if you are only making one or two chairs.

Mark the armrest for the notch that connects it to the back post. Be sure to mark this important joint carefully because it helps support the back post. You want the joint to fit snuggly. To simplify this task, clamp a scrap of 2x4 to the side frame to support the armrest while marking the notch.

Finishing for Outside Use

If you want your mahogany chair to weather to a gray patina, leave it unfinished. If you want to maintain the look of new wood, apply a good-quality clear finish.

Fabricating the Seat

When I sat in the sling seat of the replica chair, it felt like I'd need a hoist to get out. I was determined to come up with a better seat. I designed a seat with a flap on the lower backside which fastens to the lower back seat stretcher (L). This keeps both the seat back and the seat bottom stretched taut and makes the chair very comfortable to sit in.

Sewing may not be your thing, but the fabric seat for this chair is pretty basic (Photo 19, Fig. L). With the help of someone who knows how to sew, even a thick-fingered woodworker can pull off this one. Another option is to hire an upholsterer to sew it for you. They can also be a source for the outdoor canvas.

Stretching the seat is a three-step process (Photo 20 and Fig. M). Be sure the seat goes on square and snug and everything should work out fine.

Figure K:
Router Template for Armrest

Use a flexible ruler to draw the side curve. Bandsaw and belt-sand to final shape.

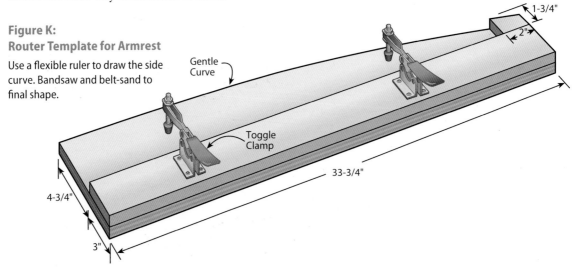

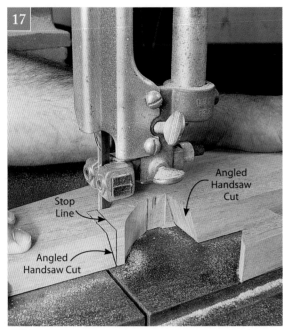

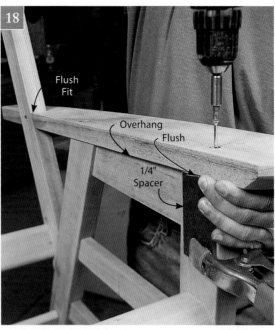

Cutting the notch in the armrest requires angled and straight cuts. First make the angle cuts with a handsaw. Then mark a stop line so you don't over cut when bandsawing the rest of the notch. The waste remains attached by a small amount of wood, but it is easily snapped off. Clean up any roughness with a chisel.

Attach the armrest. First screw it to the back post. Then twist the arm slightly to create a 1/4-in. overhang on the inside at the front leg. Counterbore for the wood plugs and drill pilot holes for the screws. Finally, glue and screw the armrest to the legs.

Figure L:
Fabric Seat Sewing Sequence

1. Cut the fabric to 22-3/4-in. wide by 77-1/2-in. long.

2. Hem both long edges with a zig-zag stitch (see illustration detail).

3. Straight-stitch the double-layer flap.

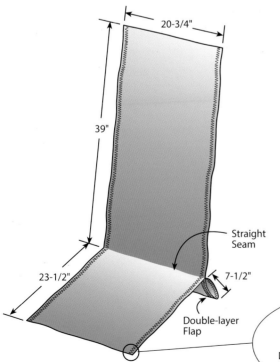

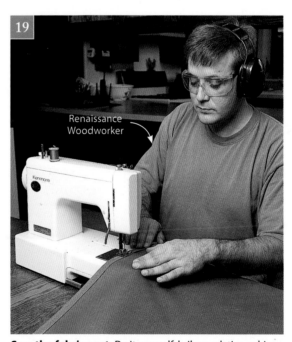

Sew the fabric seat. Do it yourself, bribe a relative or hire an upholsterer. Outdoor canvas is available in many colors and patterns. It's made to withstand sun and rain, and is mildew resistant.

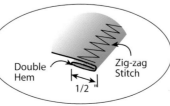

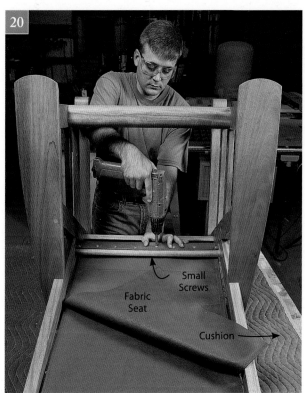

Install the fabric seat with small screws. They're easy to remove if you need to retighten or replace the seat. Stretch the fabric taut when installing it.

Figure M: Fabric Seat Mounting Sequence

1. Attach the fabric to the top seat stretcher.
2. Attach the double-layer flap to the lower seat stretcher.
3. Attach the fabric to the front seat stretcher.

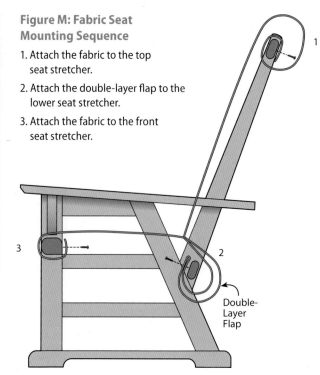

Part	Name	Qty.	Rough Dimension	Final Dimension
	Cutting List			
	Overall Dimensions: 41-1/2"H x 30"W x 33-1/2"D			
A	Front legs	2	1-1/2" x 3" x 21-1/2"	1-1/4" x 2-3/4" x 19-1/2"
B	Back legs	2	1-1/2" x 3" x 24"	1-1/4" x 2-3/4" x 22-13/16"
C	Top side rails	2	1" x 3" x 12"	3/4" x 2-3/4" x 10-13/16"*
D	Middle side rails	2	1" x 2" x 15"	3/4" x 1-3/4" x 13-7/8"*
E	Bottom side rails	2	1" x 2" x 18"	3/4" x 1-3/4" x 16-11/16"*
F	Front arched rail	1	1" x 3-1/4" x 24"	3/4" x 3" x 22-1/2"*
G	Rear leg rail	1	1" x 2-1/2" x 24"	3/4" x 2-1/2" x 22-1/2"*
H	Front seat stretcher	1	2-1/2" x 3" x 24"	2" x 2-3/4" x 22-1/2"*
J	Foot rails	2	1-1/4" x 2-1/2" x 27"	1" x 2-1/4" x 26"
K	Foot blocks	4	1-1/4" x 2-1/2" x 6-1/2"	1" x 2-1/4" x 5-1/2"
L	Back seat stretchers	2	1-1/4" x 2-3/4" x 24"	1" x 2-1/2" x 22-1/2"*
M	Back posts	2	1-1/2" x 3" x 36"	1-1/4" x 2-3/4" x 34"*
N	Armrests	2	1-1/4" x 5" x 32"	1" x 4-3/4" x 31"
P	Armrest brackets	2	1-1/2" x 2-1/4" x 6"	1-1/4" x 2" x 5"
Q	Fabric seat	1	22-3/4" x 77-1/2"	20-3/4" x 77-1/2"

* Includes tenons

EDITOR: DAVE MUNKITTRICK • ART DIRECTION: EVANGELINE EKBERG • PHOTOGRAPHY: MIKE KRIVIT • ILLUSTRATION: FRANK ROHRBACH

by LUKE HARTLE

Garden Bench

GRACEFUL, COMFORTABLE, AND BUILT TO LAST

It dawned on me the other day that every single project I've made resides in my house. Since I spend a lot of time in my back yard garden, I decided it was high time I made something to enjoy in my outdoor living space as well. This backless bench is the perfect project. The bench is now the centerpiece of my yard. Stout mortise-and-tenon joinery and naturally rot-resistant mahogany ensure that it will retain its exalted position for years to come. Traditional joinery holds the framework together; the seat slats are secured with a newer joinery technique, the Miller Dowel system (see "Miller Dowel Joinery System," page 89). The bench seemed to be the perfect project on which to try these high-tech dowels. I really liked how quick and easy they were to use compared with the traditional screw-and-plug approach.

Figure A: Exploded View

1/4"
Roundover

G

C
D
B
B
A
E
F

Detail 1: Tenon Dimensions

3/16"
1/2"
1"
B, C
1-3/4"
1"
Long Rail
and Seat Rail
1"

3/16"
1/2"
E
1-3/8"
1"
Lower Rail

Figure B: Mortise Template

Make the template from three strips of wood. The center strip is cut into three pieces and spaced to create the mortises. When you're finished, the template should be the exact length and width of the leg stock.

1/2"
11/16"
1"
1-3/4"
7-3/16"
16-1/2"
1-3/8"
5-3/16"

Detail 2: Dovetail Dimensions

3/8"
5/8"

Materials:
18 bd. ft. of 4/4 mahogany
5 bd. ft. of 8/4 mahogany

Tools:
Tablesaw, jointer, cordless drill, planer, drill press

Hardware:
28 Miller Dowels, 1X size

Cutting List			
Overall Dimensions: 55" L x 16-1/4" W x 17-1/4" H			
Part	**Qty.**	**Dimensions**	**Material**
A Leg	4	1-7/8" x 1-7/8" x 16-1/2"	8/4 mahogany
B Long rail	2	7/8" x 3" x 50-3/4"	4/4 mahogany
C Seat rail	2	7/8" x 3" x 13-3/4"	4/4 mahogany
D Spreader	2	7/8" x 3" x 14"	4/4 mahogany
E Lower rail	2	7/8" x 1-3/4" x 13-3/4"	4/4 mahogany
F Brace	1	7/8" x 1-3/4" x 51"	4/4 mahogany
G Slat	7	3/4" x 2-1/8" x 55"	4/4 mahogany

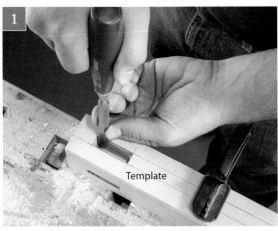

Square the corners of the mortise with a chisel before removing the template. The template serves as a guide to square the corners and ensure a perpendicular cut.

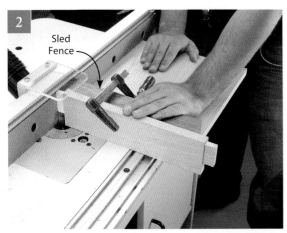

Cut the tenons on the rails with a 3/4-in.-dia. straight bit. A plywood sled with an attached hardwood fence ensures the shoulders of the tenon are cut square and keeps your hands away from the spinning bit.

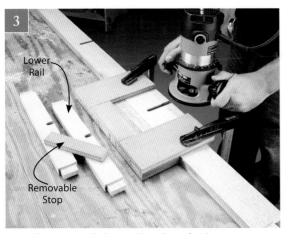

Rout the stopped-dovetail sockets for the seat supports using a simple shop-made jig. Clamp the jig to the stock and the workbench. Add a stop-block to the jig to cut the shorter sockets for the brace in the lower rails.

1. Mill all pieces to their final dimensions, except for the spreaders (D) and brace (F).
2. Make a template (Fig. B) to route the mortises.
3. To avoid mistakes, label each leg as front or back, left or right (Fig. A). Use the template to lay out the mortises.
4. Drill out the mortises on the drill press.
5. Rout the mortises in the bench legs using a template and a top-bearing pattern bit.
6. Use a chisel to square the mortise's corners.
7. Rout the tenons on the long rails (B), seat rails (C), and the lower rails (E) (Photo 2). Use a large-diameter straight-cut bit for a smooth cut.
8. Use the dovetail jig to rout the stopped-dovetail grooves in the long rails (Photo 3). Match the centerline of the socket with the centerline on the jig. Clamp everything firmly to the workbench.
9. Insert the stop block in the jig and rout the dovetail sockets in the lower rails.
10. Rough-cut the seat template pattern (Fig. C) on the bandsaw and sand smooth.
11. Rough cut the curves in the seat rails on the bandsaw. Finish the profile with the seat template and a pattern-cutting bit (Photo 4). Center the template on the rail with the back edges flush.
12. Sand all the parts to 180 grit.
13. Glue the bench frame in stages, using a waerproof glue, such as Titebond II or III. Assemble the legs, seat rails and lower rails first to create an end assembly. Then join the end assemblies with the long rails (Photo 5).

Figure C: Seat Template

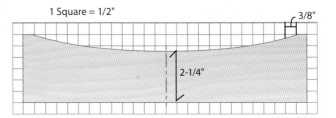

1 Square = 1/2"   3/8"

2-1/4"

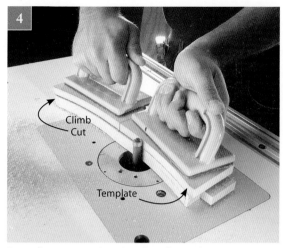

Rout the curve in the seat rails and spreaders using a template. Center the template on the rail and secure it with double-sided tape. Climb-cut the last portion of the curve first to prevent tearout.

Glue the long rails to the assembled end frames. Keep the dovetail groove opening faceup (that is, down on the bench) on the long rails. The grooves on the lower rails face the opposite direction to hide the dovetail joint.

14. Determine the exact length of the seat spreader (D) by measuring the distance between the long rails where they join the legs and adding the length of each dovetail. Cut the spreaders to length. Measuring near the legs rather than in the dovetail grooves eliminates measuring any slight bow in the long rails.

15. Measure and cut the brace (F) to length.

16. Route the tails of the dovetails on the seat spreaders and on the brace (Photo 6). Run a few test cuts on scrap lumber to get the perfect fit.

17. Use a handsaw to notch each tail so they are about 1/8 in. shorter than the sockets.

18. Rout the curves in the spreaders, as done on the seat rails in Step 11. Make sure to use the centerline for reference. Unlike the rails, the spreaders will have short flats on each end of the curve (Fig. A).

19. Sand the seat spreaders and the brace.

20. Glue in the spreaders (Photo 7). Then, flip the bench and add the brace.

21. Shape the seat slats on the router table with a 1/4-in. round-over bit.

22. Lay out all dowel locations on the seat slats (Fig. A).

23. Attach the seat slats to the bench (Photo 8). First clamp an outside slat so it overhangs the leg by 1/8 in. Run the drill at the maximum rpm level with a slow feed rate to prevent tearout around the hole.

24. Use a framing square to keep the slats' ends aligned.

25. Trim the dowel heads with a flush-cut saw.

26. Sand the slats to 180 grit.

27. Finish the bench with an outdoor finish to preserve its color and appearance or skip the finish and let it age naturally to a silver-gray color.

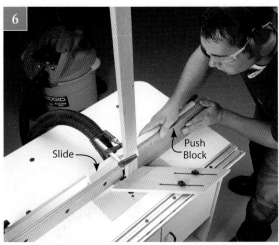

Rout the tails on the ends of the brace and the seat spreaders. Stabilize the stock using a push block with a slide attached. Fasten the slide so it runs along the top of the fence. Clamp the stock to the slide so it butts against the push block.

Glue the spreaders and the brace to the bench frame. Slide the dovetails together by hand as far as possible. Use a rubber mallet to tap the joint home. Alternate tapping each end to prevent binding.

Miller Dowel Joinery System

The Miller Dowel system combines the strength of wood joinery with the ease of a screw. Drill the hole, add the glue, tap the peg and you're finished. The secret to the dowel's success lies in its stepped design. The shoulder on the head of the dowel seats before the other shoulders do, driving the parts together much like a nail does. Horizontal ribs on the dowel absorb moisture from the glue, causing the dowel to swell in the hole and lock in place. The head of the dowel serves as a plug in the hole, but unlike traditional plugs, the Miller Dowel leaves dark-looking end grain exposed for a decorative look after the plug is sanded and finished.

Miller Dowels are available in three sizes and a wide variety of species. A companion stepped drill bit is specifically designed for each size of dowel.

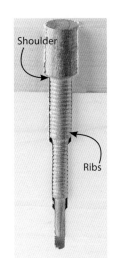

Install the slats to the bench frame using Miller Dowels. When the first board has been doweled, use a 1/4-in. spacer to set the gap between the slats. Clamp the end of each slat as you drill and dowel, working your way across the bench.

by TIM JOHNSON

Garden Chair

LOOSE TENONS JOIN PLUNGE-ROUTED MORTISES

Stylish and comfortable, these chairs are also built to last. Made of rot-resistant white oak, with robust joinery secured with weatherproof glue, they're guaranteed to become some of your garden's most cherished perennials.

We've engineered the building process so you'll be able to fit every joint using shop-made jigs and simple procedures. There are zillions of mortises, but they're all routed from only two basic setups that you'll quickly master. Making these chairs in multiples is really only a matter of physical endurance. White oak is hard and heavy!

Every structural joint consists of two plunge-routed mortises joined by a loose tenon. This variation is just as strong as traditional mortise and tenon construction and it's much easier to accomplish, particularly on this chair's angled arm and stretcher joints.

Lumber and Tools

White oak is a bargain compared to other rot-resistant hardwoods like teak and mahogany, and it's readily available in a variety of thicknesses. We used 8/4 stock for the legs (wide boards so we didn't have to glue up the blanks), 6/4 for the arms, rails and stretchers and 4/4 for the slats and tenon stock. For dimensional stability, we chose boards with straight grain. Each chair requires about 35 bd. ft. of lumber.

Routing all the mortises will give your plunge router a real workout. It must have a 1/2-in. collet, an edge guide, 2-1/8 in. of plunge capacity and the guts to plunge deep in white oak (at least 1-1/2 hp).

This project also requires a tablesaw and bandsaw, a drill press with a sanding drum and a router table. You'll need 3/8-in. and 1/2-in. straight bits for mortising, a 2-in. flush-trim bit, a 1/4-in. round-over bit and a chamfering bit. A jointer and planer are recommended, but not essential. You can have your stock milled to thickness at the lumberyard.

Building Tips

Squarely-cut blanks are essential for sound joinery and good results. Make sure your tablesaw's miter gauge makes square crosscuts. The heavy leg blanks may require a crosscut sled or an accurate chop saw.

Use templates to duplicate the shaped legs, arms and seat rails (Fig. D-G). 1/2-in.-thick MDF is excellent template material (available at most home centers for a few dollars per 2-ft. x 4-ft. sheet).

Use layout marks to guarantee that mortises and adjoining pieces go where they're supposed to go.

Plunge-rout the mortises, using a straight bit, an edge guide and clamped-on stop blocks. Mortises are either routed into the end grain using a jig, or into the long grain, using a flush-mounted support block.

Rout mortises before you cut profiles. It's much easier to fit the angled joints around the mortises than vice-versa.

Always rout from the same face so all the mortises in each piece are consistently located, even if they aren't perfectly centered. Then the joints will always line up. Simply mark all the edge-guide faces with arrows before you rout (Photo 3).

ART DIRECTION: EVANGELINE EKBERG, PATRICK HUNTER AND BARBARA PEDERSON • PHOTOGRAPHY: KRIVIT PHOTOGRAPHY • ILLUSTRATION: FRANK ROHRBACH

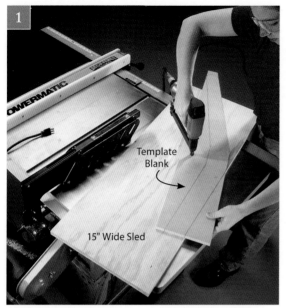

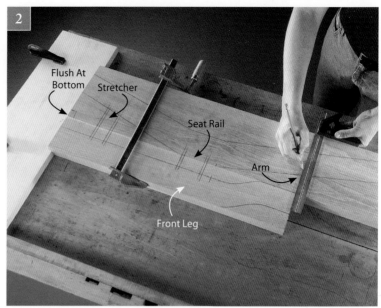

Make templates so all of your duplicated parts will be identical. Cut the templates' long, straight edges on your tablesaw, using a sled. First, set the fence and rip the sled to width. Then tack the template blank in place and run the sled through the saw.

Locate the leg mortises. Marking both blanks simultaneously guarantees that the mortises will line up. Use the top of the front leg to locate the bottom of the arm on the back leg.

Figure A: Exploded View

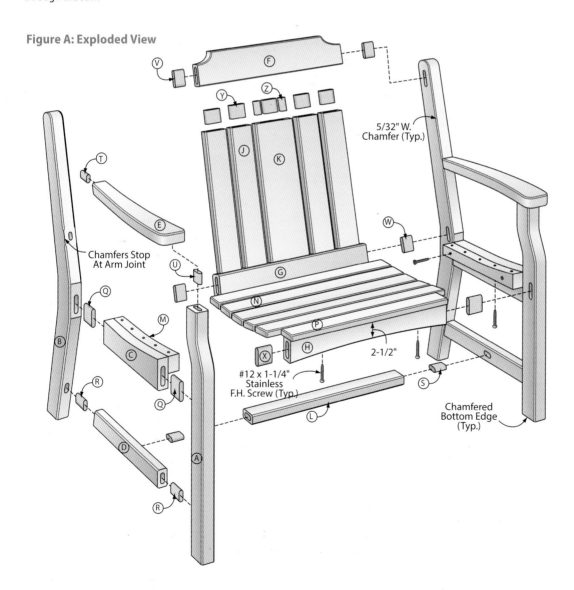

Make Templates for the Legs

Cut the leg templates from blanks that match the leg blanks (Fig. D). For the best results, saw straight portions of the templates on your tablesaw (Photo 1). Bandsaw curved shapes oversize and finish them using a sanding drum in your drill press.

To cut the back side of the back leg template on your tablesaw, you'll have to make stopped cuts from each end. Finish by cutting the remaining middle section on your bandsaw. When you cut the inside edge of the front leg template, stop the tablesaw cut at the beginning of the curve and cut the rest on the bandsaw.

Mark the Leg Blanks

Before tracing the template profiles onto the leg blanks, make sure the template and blank are aligned. The front leg template (Fig. A, Part A, and Fig. E) is easy to position, but the only reference surfaces for the rear leg (Fig. A, Part B, and Fig. D) are at the middle of the front edge and on the bottom.

After tracing the profiles, clamp the front and back leg blanks together. Then mark the locations of the mortises and outside edges of the seat rail (C), side stretcher (D) and arm (E) on the front leg blanks (Photo 2).

Mortise the Back Leg Blanks

First, adjust your router's edge guide to center the mortises on the edge of the blanks. Then rout mortises for the seat rails (Photo 3).

To rout mortises for the stretchers and arms, steps have to be cut to get the router close enough (Fig. B).

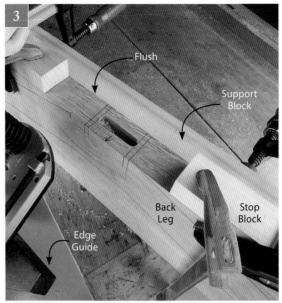

Rout mortises for the seat rails in the back legs with a plunge router. Clamp on a wide support block to stabilize the router and stop blocks to establish the ends of the mortise.

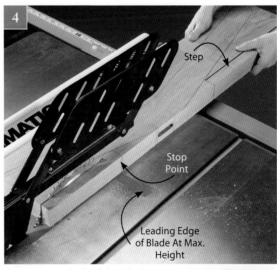

Cut steps in the back leg blanks so you can rout the arm and stretcher mortises (Fig. B, below). First, locate the blade edge and the stop point. Then make a stopped cut. Turn off the saw and back the blank out after the blade stops.

Figure B: Back Leg Blank Steps

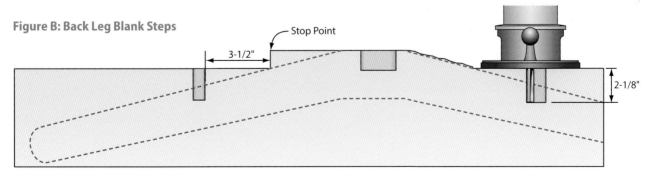

Steps must be cut to get the router motor close enough to rout the arm and stretcher mortises. Extend a line 3-1/2 in. from the upslope end of each mortise location and mark the point just before the line intersects the edge of the leg. This is the stop point for your tablesaw cut. If your router's base is over 7-in. diameter, your steps must be longer.

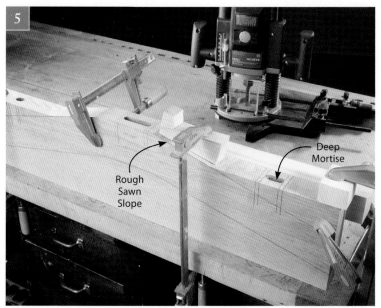

Rout super-deep mortises for the stretcher and arm from the steps, so a functional mortise remains when you cut away the waste. Rough-sawing the slope beyond the steps makes it easy to clamp on stop blocks.

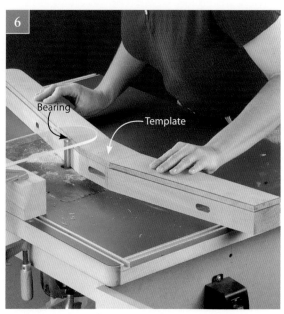

Rout the leg to its final shape with a 2-in. lathe blank and affix the template with heavy-duty double-faced tape.

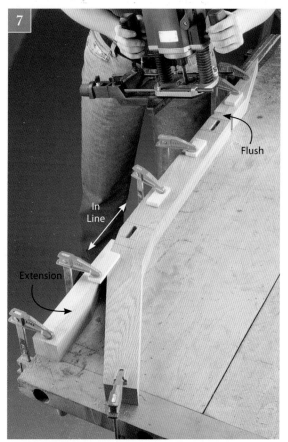

Rout mortises in the back legs for the back assembly using extensions to support the router and edge guide.

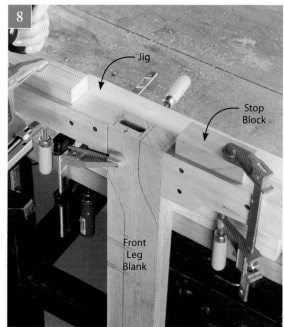

Rout mortises for the arms in the tops of the front leg blanks using a shop-made jig to support the router (Fig. C).

To create the steps, first make a stopped cut on the tablesaw (Photo 4). Finish cutting the remaining angled portion of the step on the bandsaw, making sure to stay on the outside of the line.

Extend the mortise layout lines onto the steps. Then rout 2-1/8-in.-deep mortises for the arms and stretchers (Photo 5).

Shape the Back Legs

First, rough-saw the back leg on your bandsaw to the outside edge of the pattern line. Then fasten the template with heavy-duty double-faced tape, making sure it's flush with the leg at both the bottom and front edges.

Shaping the legs requires some routing against the grain, which can cause tear-out. For the best results, mount the template on the right side of the blank (when viewed from its front edge). This setup limits against-the-grain routing to the less-visible lower portion of the leg (Photo 6).

Finish the back legs by routing the mortises for the back assembly on their inside faces, using extensions to support the router. The extensions must be as thick as the leg and clamped in line with its edge (Photo 7 and Fig. K). Be sure to adjust your edge guide before routing.

Figure C: Jig for Mortising on the End of a Piece

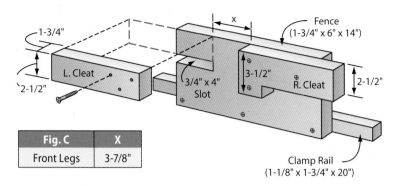

Fig. C	X
Front Legs	3-7/8"

This simple jig provides a stable platform for the router and a continuous surface for the router's edge guide. It holds the workpiece securely and easily accommodates stop blocks.

The jig consists of a fence and two 7-in.-long cleats. The cleats must be the same thickness as the workpiece and have one square corner. They mount flush with the top of the fence and are spaced so the workpiece fits between them. The fence is slotted so you can clamp the workpiece in place, flush with the top. A rail attached to the back of the fence allows you to clamp the jig securely to your workbench.

Variations of this jig, depending on the thickness and width of the workpiece, allow you to rout all of the end-grain mortises.

You can use the same fence for all the variations, just change the cleats. You'll need four pairs of cleats to complete the chair. If you plan to make more than one chair, it's a good idea to make a separate jig for each pair of cleats.

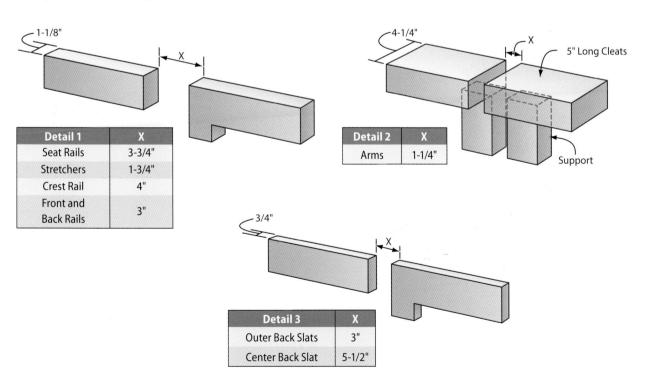

Detail 1	X
Seat Rails	3-3/4"
Stretchers	1-3/4"
Crest Rail	4"
Front and Back Rails	3"

Detail 2	X
Arms	1-1/4"

Detail 3	X
Outer Back Slats	3"
Center Back Slat	5-1/2"

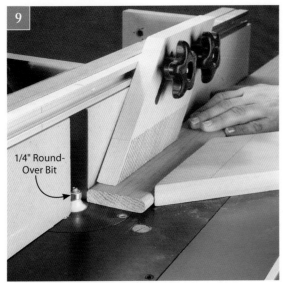

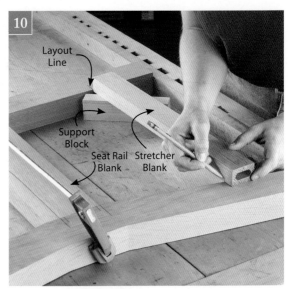

Shape loose tenon stock on the router table with a round-over bit, featherboards and a fence.

Cut the stretchers to fit after dry-assembling the legs and seat rail blank. Align the stretcher with the layout lines, butt its front end against the leg and mark the back end.

Complete the Front Legs

First, rout centered mortises for the arms, using a jig (Photo 8 and Fig. C). These mortises are offset because they're routed before the profiles are sawn.

Saw steps in the front leg blanks so you can rout the seat rail and stretcher mortises. Make stopped tablesaw cuts (on the outside edge of the pattern line) from the bottom of the blank to the start of the curve at the top. Bandsaw the remaining curved profile. Attach support and stop blocks and rout the mortises.

Rough-saw the outside curve at the top of the legs. Then mount the template (on the right side of the blanks) and rout the front leg profiles.

Real-World Angles Don't Lie

The old adage "divide and conquer" is apropos when you have to fit an assembly that includes angled joints, like the chair sides. Instead of cutting all the parts based on a cutting list, fit the joints one at a time.

Dry-clamping the square joints between the seat rail blank and the legs gives you all the information you need to fit the angled joints. The angle for the back end of the side stretcher is the same as the angle between the bottom of the seat rail blank and the leg. The arm's back-end angle is the same as the one between the seat rail blank and the *top* of the leg.

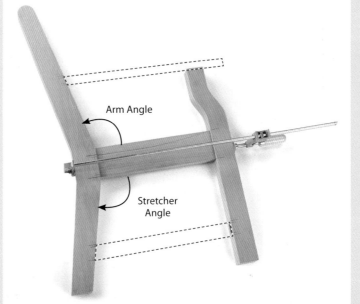

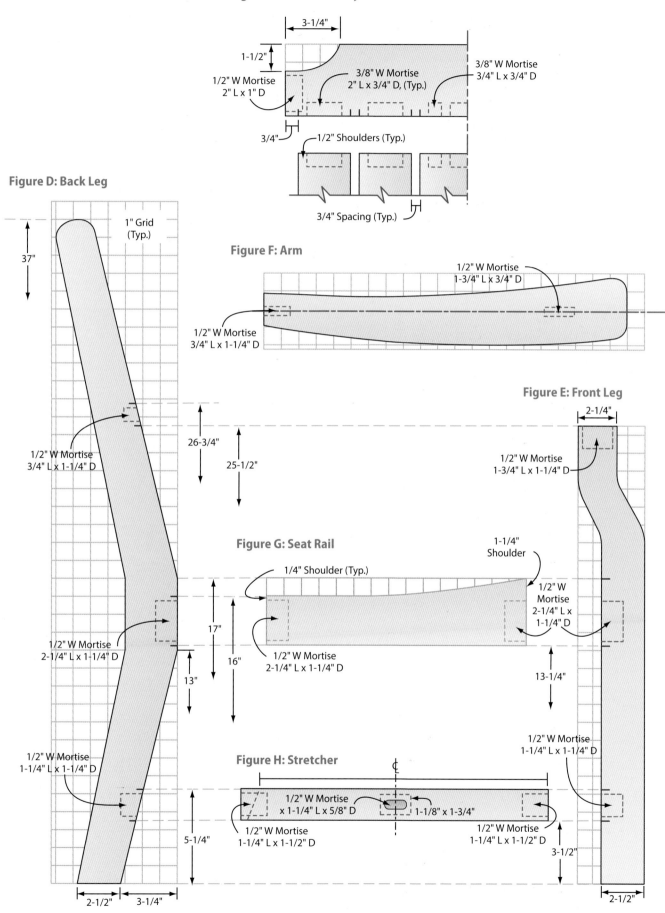

Figure J: Back Assembly

3-1/4"

1-1/2"

1/2" W Mortise
2" L x 1" D

3/8" W Mortise
2" L x 3/4" D, (Typ.)

3/8" W Mortise
3/4" L x 3/4" D

3/4"

1/2" Shoulders (Typ.)

3/4" Spacing (Typ.)

Figure D: Back Leg

1" Grid
(Typ.)

37"

Figure F: Arm

1/2" W Mortise
1-3/4" L x 3/4" D

1/2" W Mortise
3/4" L x 1-1/4" D

Figure E: Front Leg

2-1/4"

1/2" W Mortise
1-3/4" L x 1-1/4" D

1/2" W Mortise
3/4" L x 1-1/4" D

26-3/4"

25-1/2"

Figure G: Seat Rail

1-1/4"
Shoulder

1/4" Shoulder (Typ.)

1/2" W
Mortise
2-1/4" L x
1-1/4" D

1/2" W Mortise
2-1/4" L x 1-1/4" D

17"

16"

1/2" W Mortise
2-1/4" L x 1-1/4" D

13"

13-1/4"

1/2" W Mortise
1-1/4" L x 1-1/4" D

1/2" W Mortise
1-1/4" L x 1-1/4" D

Figure H: Stretcher

1/2" W Mortise
x 1-1/4" L x 5/8" D

1-1/8" x 1-3/4"

5-1/4"

1/2" W Mortise
1-1/4" L x 1-1/2" D

1/2" W Mortise
1-1/4" L x 1-1/2" D

3-1/2"

2-1/2" 3-1/4"

2-1/2"

Locate the arm mortise. First, cut the bevel on the back of the arm blank. Install the loose tenon and clamp the blank to the back leg. Then transfer the layout lines for the mortise from the front leg to the arm.

Rout the mortise in the bottom face of the arm blank. It's centered, just like the mortise in the end.

Glue the side assembly together standing up, so it's easy to clamp and clean glue squeeze-out. Center the clamps on the joints using angled blocks to direct pressure squarely on the angled joints.

Glue the back slats and rails. To keep the wide center slat from cracking, leave its outer tenons unglued.

Mortise the Seat Rail, Stretcher and Arm Blanks

The seat rails, side and center stretchers (L) are all the same thickness, so they can all be routed with the same set of cleats mounted on the end-mortising jig (Fig. C, Detail 1).

First, rout 1-1/4-in.-deep mortises in the seat rail blanks (Fig. G), centered between the faces and offset from the top edge. Be sure to rout both ends from the same face.

Reposition the right-hand cleat and rout 1-1/2-in.-deep mortises in the stretcher blanks (Fig. H).

Mortise one end of both arm blanks (Fig. F). This job requires its own set of extra-wide cleats and support blocks (Fig. C, Detail 2).

Make the Loose Tenons

Individual 1/2-in.-thick tenons (Q through X) are cut from long pre-milled blanks. First, plane 2-ft. lengths of straight-grained stock to 1/2-in. thickness and rip them to width. Then shape the edges on your router table (Photo 9).

Your tenon stock should slip in and out of the mortises without binding (too tight) or rattling (too loose). Cut the tenons about 1/16-in. short and test-fit the seat rail and stretcher joints. Adjust the fit by shaving the tenons or wedging the mortises until the adjoining pieces line up with the layout lines.

Fit the Angled Joints

First, find the cutting angle for the stretchers (see Real-World Angles Don't Lie, page 96). Then transfer this angle to your tablesaw's miter gauge using a sliding bevel square. Mark the stretcher for the angled cut (Photo 10) and cut it to length.

Find the cutting angle for the back end of the arm. Tilt the blade to this angle. Reset your miter gauge to 90 degrees and cut the back end of the arm blank.

Rout mortises in the side stretchers for the center stretcher (Fig. H). Then assemble the sides and install the arm blanks so you can locate and rout the front mortises (Photos 11 and 12).

Assemble the Sides

Mount the arm blanks with tenons installed in both mortises. Trace the arm's profile onto the blanks while holding the template (Fig. F) against the back leg, flush on both sides. Remove the arm blanks and rough-saw them. Then attach the template and rout the profile on the router table using the flush-trim bit.

Rough-saw and rout both seat rail blanks using the template (Fig. G). Chamfer all the exposed sharp edges on the arms, legs, seat rails and stretchers. The chamfers stop above and below the arm joint on the back legs. Chamfer only the bottom edges of the seat rails. Don't chamfer the ends of pieces that butt at joints. Then glue each side assembly together (Photo 13).

Assemble the Back

Rout 1-in.-deep mortises in the ends of the crest rail blank (F) and lower back rail (G), using the jig (Fig. C, Detail 1). These mortises are offset (Fig. J and Fig. K). Mortise the ends of the front rail (H) now as well.

The 3/4-in.-thick back slats (J and K) require thinner mortises and tenons (Y and Z), but the plunge routing procedure remains the same. Draw layout lines on the rails (Fig. J), clamp on a fence and stop blocks, set the edge guide and always rout from the same face.

Make sure the back slats are the right length. Dry-clamp the crest and lower back rails in place between the glued-up sides and verify the distance between them. Then mortise the ends of the slats using the jig (Fig. C, Detail 3).

Figure K: Mortise Locations for Back Assembly and Front Rail

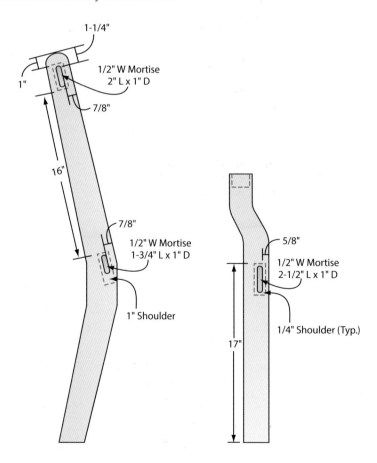

1-1/4"
1/2" W Mortise
2" L x 1" D
1"
7/8"
16"
7/8"
1/2" W Mortise
1-3/4" L x 1" D
1" Shoulder
5/8"
1/2" W Mortise
2-1/2" L x 1" D
17"
1/4" Shoulder (Typ.)

Bandsaw the curved profile on the ends of the crest rail and smooth it on your drill press with the sanding drum. Next, chamfer all the edges (but not the ends) of the rails and slats.

Make tenon stock to fit the 3/8-in.-thick mortises, using the 1/4-in. round-over bit, lowered slightly, to round the ends. For this 28-mortise glue-up, give yourself some wiggle room by making the tenons slightly undersize (see Oops!, below). Then rely on your layout lines to position the slats when you glue the back assembly together (Photo 14). After clamping, measure the diagonals and make any necessary adjustments to make sure this assembly is square.

Glue the Frame Together

Dry-fit the chair frame and clamp it together. Then determine the exact length of the center stretcher by measuring between the side stretchers. Cut it to fit.

Disassemble the chair and draw the shallow arch on the bottom of the front rail. Flex a yardstick or thin piece of scrap to use as a pattern. Bandsaw the arch and smooth it with the sanding drum.

Glue the chair frame together on a level surface (Photo 15). Use your layout lines to make sure all the rails are in position. After clamping, measure the inside diagonals of the seat opening to check for square.

Install the Seat

Make the seat subrails (M) and the seat slats (N and P). Screw the subrails to the seat rails. Glue and screw the front slat to the front rail, flush with the back edges of the legs. Then install the rest of the slats (Photo 16).

The Finish

White oak is rot resistant, but left unprotected, your chair will turn gray and may feel somewhat rough, because exposure to moisture will raise the grain. If it stays damp for extended periods, mildew can be a problem. You can get rid of mildew and restore the oak's natural color by treating it with a deck renewal product. Light sanding will smooth the surface.

We chose an outdoor oil finish because it makes the oak come alive with color. It also offers a layer of protection against the elements, including mildew. You should plan to apply (brush on/wipe off) several coats of this finish every year.

The most durable exterior finish is spar varnish, which also gives the oak a pretty color. It's a brushed-on, high-gloss finish that will last for several years without peeling or cracking. You'll have to sand it down before recoating.

Oops!

My loose tenons fit the mortises perfectly, but gluing the back assembly, with its 14 tenons and 28 mortises, turned out to be a nightmare. By the time I spread glue on all the parts, the pieces wouldn't go together whether I clamped, hammered or prayed!

I didn't realize that, given the chance, water-soluble glue can make the wood expand enough to effect the way joints fit. I couldn't have worked any faster, so I should have made the tenons a bit thinner. A good

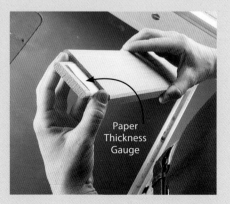

My loose tenons were too tight!

rule of thumb for a lengthy assembly like this one is to test-fit the joints with paper wrapped around the tenons. This amount of tolerance (two thicknesses of paper) allows enough slack to get the assembly together, without seriously weakening the glue joints, as long as you remember to remove the paper!

Paper Thickness Gauge

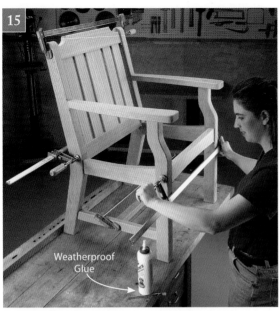

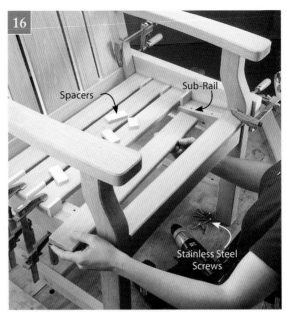

Glue the frame together. To ensure even clamping pressure on all the joints, center your clamps, keep them level and tighten them sequentially, one twist at a time.

Install the seat slats, using spacers and a clamped-on board for alignment. Clamp the slats and fasten them from underneath, through predrilled, countersunk holes in the subrails.

Cutting List
Overall Dimensions 27-1/2" W x 25-1/2" D x 37-1/2" H

Part	Name	Number	Blank Dimensions	Final Dimensions
A	Front Leg	2	1-3/4" x 3-7/8" x 25-1/2" **	1-3/4" x 3-7/8" x 25-1/2"
B	Back Leg	2	1-3/4" x 7-1/4" x 39" **	1-3/4" x 7" x 37"
C	Seat Rail	2	1-1/8" x 3-3/4" x 15" **	1-1/8" x 3-3/4" x 15"
D	Side Stretcher	2	1-1/8" x 1-3/4" x 17-3/4" **	1-1/8" x 1-3/4" x cut to length
E	Arm	2	1-1/4" x 4-1/4" x 22" **	1-1/4" x 3-7/8" x 21"
F	Crest Rail	1	1-1/8" X 4" X 22" **	1-1/8" x 4" x 22"
G	Lower Back Rail	1		1-1/8" x 3" x 22"
H	Front Seat Rail *	1		1-1/8" x 3" x 22"
J	Outer Back Slats	4		3/4" x 3" x 16"
K	Center Back Slat	1		3/4" x 5-1/2" x 16"
L	Center Stretcher	1	1-1/8" x 1-3/4" x 23" **	1-1/8" x 1-3/4" x 22-5/8"
M	Seat SubRail	2		1-1/8" x 2-1/4" x 15"
N	Seat Slats	5		13/16" x 2-5/8" x 25-1/2"
P	Front Seat Slat	1		13/16" x 2-5/8" x 22"
Q	Seat Rail Tenons	4	1/2" x 2-1/4" x 24"	1/2" x 2-1/4" x 2-1/2" ***
R	Side Stretcher Tenons	4	1/2" x 1-1/4" x 24"	1/2" x 1-1/4" x 2-3/4" ***
S	Center Stretcher Tenons	2	use side stretcher tenon blank	1/2" x 1-1/4" x 2-1/8" ***
T	Back Arm Tenons	2	1/2" x 3/4" x 24"	1/2" x 3/4" x 2-1/2" ***
U	Front Arm Tenons	2	1/2" x 1-3/4" x 24"	1/2" x 1-3/4" x 2" ***
V	Crest Rail Tenons	2	1/2" x 2" x 24"	1/2" x 2" x 2" ***
W	Lower Back Rail Tenons	2	use front arm tenon blank	1/2" x 1-3/4" x 2" ***
X	Front Rail Tenons	2	1/2" x 2-1/2" x 24"	1/2" x 2-1/2" x 2" ***
Y	Back Slat Tenons	10	3/8" x 2" x 24"	3/8" x 2" x 1-1/2" ***
Z	Center Slat Tenons	4	3/8" x 5/8" x 24"	3/8" x 5/8" x 1-1/2" ***

* Arched bottom edge rises 1/2" at center
** Blank must be squarely cut
*** Cut 1/16-in. short of actual measured length

by TOM CASPAR

Outdoor Rietveld Chair

AN ICON OF MODERN DESIGN BECOMES A COMFORTABLE, EASY-TO-BUILD OUTDOOR PROJECT

In 1918 the Dutch cabinetmaker Gerrit Rietveld reduced the idea of a chair to a 3D grid of painted sticks and boards. His revolutionary design became one of the most famous pieces of 20th-century furniture—the Red-Blue chair.

Let's take a new look at it. Although his chair appears easy to put together, getting all those sticks precisely located is tough, especially if you have only two hands. And all the pieces look alike! To make this jigsaw puzzle simpler to put together, I've figured out a building system based on two plywood boards and a few spacing blocks. If, like most people, you want to build a bunch of chairs instead of just one, this system is the ticket. Once you've built the first chair, the rest will be easy as ABC.

The Design

I've revised Rietveld's elegant design to make a chair that's stronger, easier to build, more comfortable to sit in and rugged enough to put outdoors. I've used screws instead of Rietveld's dowels to hold it together, increased the size of the sticks and added a stretcher. We tested our chair with both large and small people, and it gets two thumbs up for comfort. Some said it was perfect for leaning back and playing video games!

Tools and Materials

Building this chair requires only a minimum of tools and experience. You'll need a tablesaw, planer and router to mill the wood, and a #2 square-drive bit for your drill to put it together. That's it. A drill press and a router table are helpful, but not necessary.

Honduras mahogany is a good choice for this chair. It's easy to cut, sands quickly and is weatherproof, even without a finish. Alternative woods include teak and white oak. Softwoods that are often used for outdoor furniture like cedar, redwood and cypress are probably too weak for this chair and do not hold screws well. If mahogany is too pricey for you, I've scaled the chair so you could use tough construction lumber such as Douglas fir or Southern yellow pine instead. Both are available at most lumberyards and should hold up outdoors if painted.

One chair requires about 12 board feet of 6/4 wood and about 10 board feet of 4/4 wood.

If your chair will be outdoors, use stainless steel screws and water-resistant glue. Unlike stainless steel, standard screws will leave unsightly stains on the wood. I prefer Titebond II glue for kiln-dried hardwoods such as mahogany, but if you're using construction lumber, polyurethane glue (Gorilla Glue, for example) would be a better choice because it works well on wood with a high moisture content.

Figure A: Guide Block for Screw Holes
The overlapping joints in this chair are screwed and glued together. This block lays out diagonal pairs of screw holes in five rails (D). Use one side to mark either end of a rail. Flip the block over to mark the other end. Then the two diagonals will run in opposite directions.

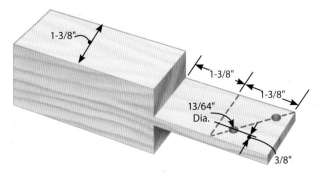

1-3/8"
1-3/8"
1-3/8"
13/64" Dia.
3/8"

by JONATHAN BENSON

Rustic Chair

MAKE A CHAIR IN A DAY USING GREEN WOOD SAPLINGS

You can make a pretty good case for bending and attaching green wood sticks as the second oldest wood-furniture making method—after coming upon a fallen log, and sitting. Today, this type of furniture is labeled "rustic," so exposed nails, screws and other hardware are acceptable for joining the individual pieces. Larger pieces can be joined using mortise-and-tenon joints cut by hand, a drill or a commercially available tenon cutter. Nails or leather straps also work well for joining the wood together.

Building this child's chair (see Fig. A) is a good introduction to rustic chairmaking. It's also a lesson in the great bending properties of willow. With rustic furniture, there are often no drawings or set plans. The shapes and sizes of the wood at hand and the maker's eye are often the determining factors when creating a design. A few basic dimensions are important, however. For rustic chairs, they include the height, width and depth of the seat. (see Fig. B). As this chair is designed for a child, it's smaller than an adult-size chair. But both chairs are made the same way.

EDITOR: TIM JOHNSON • PHOTOS COURTESY OF FOX CHAPEL PUBLISHING

Working with Green Wood

Green wood is either freshly sawn or has not undergone any formal drying process. It retains moisture and the wood's natural resins, which makes it easier to bend than wood that has been thoroughly dried. Alder, birch, beech, hickory, and willow are commonly used to make bentwood rustic furniture. Willow may have the best qualities of all because it bends easily, stays in place, and the bark usually doesn't come off when the wood dries. It can also be a reliable source of material—a good stand of willows near a creek or river will yield new saplings year after year.

Saplings work best for bending, because they are relatively straight and have few offshoots and leaves (Photo 1). That makes them easy to prepare. Use saplings and small branches to construct bent components, such as the arms and seat of this chair. Use thicker branches to construct the support structure.

When you cut live branches and saplings, it's best to use them right away, before they have a chance to dry out. The sticks can be wrapped in plastic and stored for a while, but they'll continue to dry. Mildew can also be a problem.

For the bent pieces in this chair, I cut willow and Osage-orange saplings that were about 1" in diameter at their thickest. The structural members were cut from branches of willow and Osage-orange and were slightly more than 1" in diameter. This chair's structural frames hold the bent elements in tension, which adds much strength to its overall structure. To create bent pieces that are uniformly shaped, you must pre-bend the thick end of each piece by hand or over the edge of a bench. Otherwise, the pieces will tend to bend more where they are thinner and less where they are thickest, resulting in uneven curves. Use galvanized nails (with heads) to fasten the pieces. Some joints could be wrapped with leather to add strength and detail.

Willow saplings and branches about 1" in diameter make suitable bending material. Slightly larger branches are best for structural members.

Start by making a pair of frames. One frame supports the seat; the other frame supports the legs. Using a slightly curved branch for the front of the seat frame makes the seat more comfortable.

Nail each frame together after pre-drilling each hole, to avoid splitting the wood. Orient the pieces firmly against the bench, so the force of the hammer is directly transferred through the nail to the bench.

Nail the first arm inside the leg frame.

Bend the arm inside the opposite rail and nail it in place. Then trim the ends. This chair has a total of four bent arms. Pre-bending the branches before installation makes their curves more uniform.

Figure A: Rustic Child's Chair

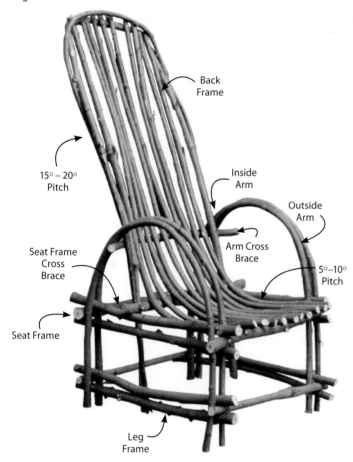

Back Frame

15° – 20° Pitch

Inside Arm

Outside Arm

Arm Cross Brace

5°–10° Pitch

Seat Frame Cross Brace

Seat Frame

Leg Frame

Install the second inside arm. The remaining two arms are attached on the outside of the frame.

Install the seat frame by nailing it between the four arms. Angle the frame 5° to 10° to the back, to make the seat more comfortable. Here I've installed one of the outside arms to help with positioning.

Figure B: Common Chair Measurements

	Barstool	Childs	Dining (side)	Dining (arm)	Easy	Kitchen	Stool	Rocker
Seat Width	17"	18"	19"	24"	25"	19"	12"	20"
Seat Depth	17"	15"	19"	18"	26"	19"	12"	26"
Seat Height	30"	12"	18"	18"	17"	19"	27"	16"
Back Height	42"	40"	36"	36"	31"	34"		42"

Construct the back frame by bending two long branches into a loop and threading them through a pair of nailed-on cross braces. The brace on the seat frame determines the seat's depth. The arm brace determines the pitch of the back—usually between 15° and 20°. Slightly bending this brace makes the back more comfortable.

Create the back's U-shaped frame by wiring together two long branches, so the thick end of one branch is attached to the thin end of the other. The wire helps the two branches bend uniformly. Nail the back frame in position. Then remove the wire.

Fill in the seat and back to complete the chair. Pre-bend the first branch to create a comfortable seat and back, after passing it between the two pieces that form the back's frame. Snug the branch against one of the inside arms. Make sure the branch is vertical and then nail it to the front rail, cross braces and back frame.

Install the remaining branches. Pre-bend the second branch and snug it against the opposite arm. Then work from both sides toward the center. Space the branches as far apart or as close together as you want, depending on your design and how many branches you have. These branches are spaced about 3/4" apart.

by JOHN ENGLISH

Hammock Stand

MAKE BENT LAMINATIONS ON A BIG SCALE

One sweeping curve, 18-ft. long: that's the essence of this dramatic stand. Making up that curve are dozens of thin pieces of construction-grade redwood, all glued together to make an extremely strong beam.

The beam is composed of three identical pieces: two are butted end-to-end to make the lower curve, while a third piece bolted on top binds the two together. I'll show you how to build an inexpensive bending form to create the three sections, how to cut the laminations and glue them together, and how to make the beam's edges smooth and even.

You'll need twelve 10 ft. redwood 2x4s to make the laminations. (You could substitute western red cedar, as long as the pieces are fairly free of knots.) You'll also need about 62 lineal feet of 2x4's, including one 14-footer, to make the stand's other parts.

Build the Bending Form

1. To build the form, you'll need one 4 ft. x 9 ft. sheet of 1/2-in.-thick house siding (hardboard or plywood). You'll also need two 1x4s (one 10-footer and one 12-footer) to make a very large beam compass, also known as a trammel. Screw or clamp the 10-footer to the siding (Photo 1 and Fig. B).

2. Attach the 12-ft. 1x4 to the end of the 10-ft. 1x4 with a bolt and nut, so the 12-footer will pivot as a swinging arm. Drill a hole to fit a pencil in the other end of the arm. Screw a short piece of 1x4 to the bottom of the arm, just inside the pencil hole, so the arm glides easily across the siding. Draw the arc, then disassemble the trammel.

3. Cut the arc using a jigsaw. Screw the trammel's 10-footer to the long, straight side of the siding, to stiffen it.

4. Cut 68 blocks from 2x4 stock (you'll need 18 lineal feet; Fig. C). Drill a 1/8-in.-dia. pilot hole in the center of each block. Glue and screw the blocks in pairs along the curved edge of the siding (Photo 2). Position each block so that the middle of its top edge is flush with the curve.

5. Cut two strips from the discarded portion of the siding. Glue and screw the strips to the top of the 2x4 blocks, butting the strips end-to-end (Photo 3). Apply wide masking tape to the form's top surface to prevent the laminations from adhering after a glue-up. Wrap the tape over the form's edges and down an inch on both sides.

Resaw the Laminations

6. Make laminations for the beams (A, B) by resawing redwood 2x4s (Photo 4). You can do this using a bandsaw, but it's just as easy using a tablesaw equipped with a rip blade. Attach a 3-3/4-in.-high subfence to your saw. Clamp or screw a board on top of the subfence to prevent the 2x4s from climbing up the blade. Position the subfence about 7/16 in. away from the blade in order to rip the 2x4 into three equal pieces. Raise the blade 2 in. above the table. Install a featherboard to hold the stock tight against the subfence.

7. Make the first cut. Turn the 2x4 over and make a second cut. Turn the 2x4 end-for-end and make a third cut. This cut releases one lamination. Set the boards aside and repeat these three cuts on all of your 2x4s. Move the featherboard toward the fence and make the fourth and final cut in each board, releasing two more laminations.

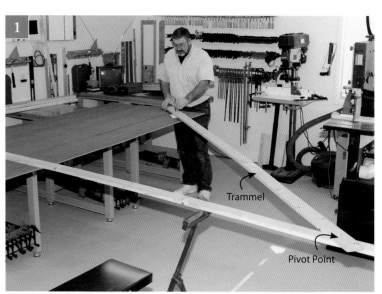

The stand's curved beams are made of many thin laminations, glued together over a bending form. Begin making the form by laying out an arc on a large sheet of hardboard siding material, using a long board as a trammel.

Cut the hardboard using a jigsaw, then fasten pairs of short 2x4 blocks along the entire curve.

Screw a long piece of hardboard to the blocks. This creates a wide support for the laminations. You're done making the bending form.

Caution: You must remove your guard for this operation. Be careful.

Resaw 10-ft.-long redwood 2x4's into three pieces to make the laminations.

Plane the laminations 1/4 in. thick, then sort through the pile to select the best-looking pieces. Use these for the top and bottom faces of each beam.

Spread glue on the laminations with a dense-foam roller

8. Allow the laminations to acclimate in your shop for a week or so, then plane them 1/4 in. thick.

Glue The Beams

9. Sort through the laminations and select the most attractive pieces for the top and bottom of each beam (Photo 5). Strips with knots or defects are OK for middle pieces.

10. Use a weatherproof glue for the laminations. I prefer Titebond III because it allows very little cold creep (which means the edges of the laminations will stay even over time). A dense-foam roller works well for spreading the glue. Keep the roller in a large, sealed plastic bag between applications, so you won't have to wash it out every time. Select four laminations and pour glue in a wavy pattern on top of three of them. Spread the glue thick enough to obscure the wood's grain pattern (Photo 6).

11. Clamp the four laminations to the bending form (Photo 7). Place blocks under each clamp head to avoid denting the top lamination. Before applying final pressure, align the laminations with quick-action ratcheting clamps. Start at the center of the curve and work towards each end, placing a clamp on every other 2x4 block attached to the form. Alternate the clamps side-to-side to evenly distribute pressure. Inspect for gaps between the laminations before you let the assembly dry overnight. Use more clamps to close gaps as needed.

12. Repeat this procedure three times to complete one beam, which contains a total of twelve laminations. To remove the beam from the form, score through the glue run-off with a utility knife and push the beam sideways. Avoid prying it up. Glue together two more beams the same width and length.

Dress The Beams

13. Use a paint scraper and jack plane to remove the dried glue from one side of each beam. Make sure that the side is square to the top (Photo 8). Scrape glue from the opposite side and run the beams through the planer. Make all three beams the same thickness.

Figure A: Exploded View

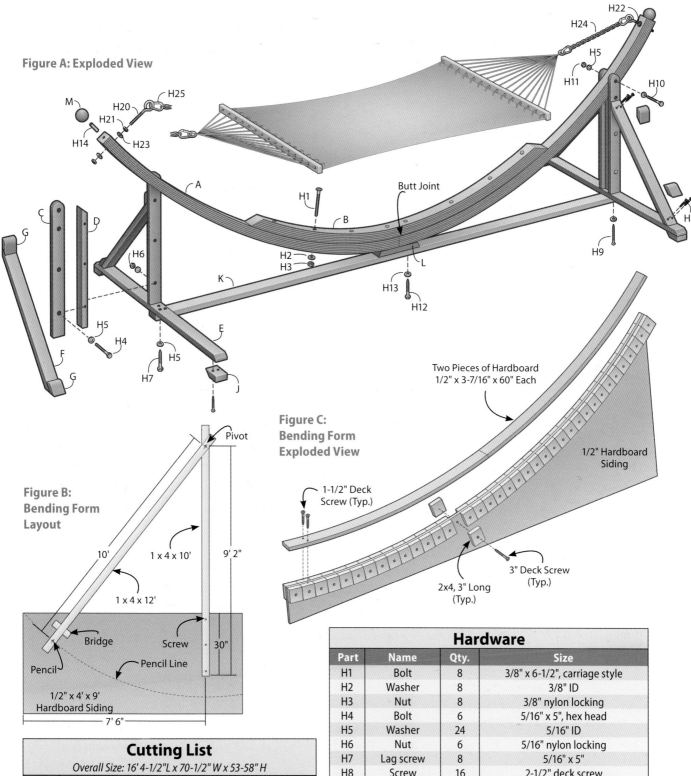

Butt Joint

**Figure B:
Bending Form
Layout**

Pivot

10'

1 x 4 x 10'

9' 2"

1 x 4 x 12'

Bridge

Screw

Pencil

Pencil Line

30"

1/2" x 4' x 9'
Hardboard Siding

7' 6"

**Figure C:
Bending Form
Exploded View**

Two Pieces of Hardboard
1/2" x 3-7/16" x 60" Each

1/2" Hardboard
Siding

1-1/2" Deck
Screw (Typ.)

2x4, 3" Long
(Typ.)

3" Deck Screw
(Typ.)

Cutting List
Overall Size: 16' 4-1/2"L x 70-1/2" W x 53-58" H

Part	Name	Qty.	Th x W x L
A	Bottom beam	2	3" x 3-1/8" x 112" (a)
B	Top beam	1	3" x 3-1/8" x 112" (a)
C	Post	4	1-1/2" x 3-1/2" x 36"
D	Leg spacer	2	1-1/2" x 3-1/8" x 36"
E	Base	2	1-1/2" x 3-1/2" x 70-1/2"
F	Brace	4	1-1/2" x 3-1/2" x 40"
G	Corner block	8	1-1/2" x 3-1/2" x 4-1/2"
J	Foot	4	1-1/2" x 3-1/2" x 4-1/2"
K	Stretcher	1	1-1/2" x 3-1/2" x 168"
L	Beam spacer	1	1-1/2" x 3-1/2" x 15"
M	Ball	2	3" dia.

(a) composed of 12 laminations; each lamination
is 1/4" x 3-1/2" x 120"

Hardware

Part	Name	Qty.	Size
H1	Bolt	8	3/8" x 6-1/2", carriage style
H2	Washer	8	3/8" ID
H3	Nut	8	3/8" nylon locking
H4	Bolt	6	5/16" x 5", hex head
H5	Washer	24	5/16" ID
H6	Nut	6	5/16" nylon locking
H7	Lag screw	8	5/16" x 5"
H8	Screw	16	2-1/2" deck screw
H9	Screw	2	6" deck screw
H10	Bolt	2	5/16" x 6", hex head
H11	Nut	2	5/16" nylon locking
H12	Lag screw	4	1/4" x 5"
H13	Washer	4	1/4" ID
H14	Dowel	2	5/16" x 2"
H20	Eyebolt	2	Parts from a 1/2" x 13" turnbuckle
H21	Nut	1	1/2", standard thread
H22	Nut	1	1/2", left-hand thread
H23	Washer	2	1/2", fender style
H24	Chain	2	36" each, 500 lb. minimum rating
H25	Link	4	3/8" spring snap

Clamp four laminations to the bending form, then let the glue cure. Each beam consists of twelve laminations.

Make three beams. Level and square one side of each beam using a jack plane. Then mill the beams to final thickness using a planer.

Try Square

The stand's bottom curve consists of two beams butted end-to-end, with the third beam fastened on top. Clamp the top beam to one of the bottom beams and drill holes through both pieces. Fasten the beams with carriage bolts.

From here, building the stand is just a matter of screwing, bolting, or nailing pieces together. These pieces form one of the two leg stands supporting the beams.

14. Cut both ends of two beams at 90 degrees using a miter saw with added outboard support. These pieces become the bottom beams (A). Cut the other beam's ends at 45 degrees. This piece becomes the top beam (B).

15. Mark the center of the top beam and clamp it to one of the bottom beams (Fig. A). Use a 3/8-in.-dia. extra-long drill bit to bore four holes through both pieces (Photo 9). Assemble the beams using carriage bolts, washers and nuts. Clamp the other bottom beam to this assembly, drill holes, and bolt the pieces together, making one long beam.

16. Chamfer both ends of the long beam using a block plane or a bearing-guided chamfering bit in a router. Prepare two redwood balls (M) to decorate the beam's ends. (These balls are available at most home centers. They're used on decks.) Clamp each ball between the jaws of a handscrew and clamp this assembly to a drill

press table. Bore a 5/16-in.-dia. hole 1 in. deep into each ball. Glue dowels into the holes. Bore a matching hole in each end of the beam and glue the balls in place.

Build the Leg Stands

17. Cut the leg posts (C) to size and mark their round tops. Cut the ends using a bandsaw and smooth them using a belt sander. Joint and rip two leg spacers (D) the same width as the beam. Miter the top of each spacer at 45 degrees. Counterbore holes in the leg posts using a Forstner bit for the leg-to-spacer bolts and the leg-to-beam bolts. Fasten two posts to each spacer.

18. Cut the base pieces (E) to length and chamfer the ends using a miter saw. Center the leg-and-spacer assembly on each base and mark the location of the lag screws that go into the end of each leg post. Counterbore and pre-drill

Reinforce the triangular braces of each leg stand with short blocks, glued and nailed in place.

Connect the leg stands with a 14-ft.-long stretcher. Use extra-long deck screws to fasten the stretcher to the posts.

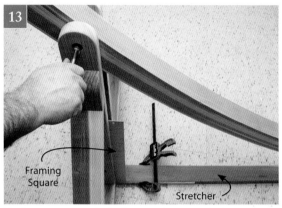

The beams nest inside the leg stands. Fasten the beam to each stand with a single long bolt. This allows the joint to flex under pressure.

As the last step, fasten the beams to the stretcher in the middle of the stand.

holes for the screws and washers. Fasten the legs to the bases (Photo 10).

19. Cut braces (F) with 45 degree ends to stiffen this assembly. Fasten them to the posts. Reinforce these joints with corner blocks (G). Make the blocks in pairs, starting with 12 in.-long pieces mitered at both ends. Cut the blocks to length, then bandsaw and sand their rounded ends. Install the blocks with glue and galvanized finish nails (Photo 11). Screw and glue a pair of feet (J) to the bottom of each leg base.

20. Make the stretcher (K) from a 14 ft. 2x4. Counterbore holes and drill pilot holes in the center of the stretcher for the stretcher-to-beam bolts. Attach the stretcher to the legs (Photo 12). Use a framing square to make sure that each leg is 90 degrees to the stretcher (Photo 13).

21. Cut the beam spacer (L) to length and chamfer its ends. Leave a blunt edge about 1/2 in. wide. Place the spacer in the center of the stretcher. Drop the beam in place between the leg posts. It should rest on top of the leg spacers (D). If it doesn't, adjust the beam spacer's thickness or the length of the stretcher (K). Center the beam on the stretcher and clamp it so that it rests in the same location on both leg posts. Attach the beam to the legs. Raise one end of the hammock stand and support it with some low sawhorses or boxes. Fasten the stretcher and spacer to the beam (Photo 14).

Hang the Hammock

22. This stand will handle hammocks up to 14-ft. long (most hammocks are 10 to 12 ft. long). Look for a hammock with spreader bars at the ends—it will sag less in the middle and is easier to climb into.

EDITOR: TIM JOHNSON • PHOTOGRAPHY: JASON ZENTNER • ILLUSTRATION: FRANK ROHRBACH

by BRAD HOLDEN

Handsome Patio Planter

STRONG, SIMPLE JOINERY PROVIDES LASTING BEAUTY

If you've been thinking about beautifying your patio, and you want to do it in a weekend, I've got just the thing. This sturdy planter is made from readily available materials with simple joinery, waterproof glue, and exterior stain for maximum durability.

You'll need two 12-ft. cedar 5/4 x 6 deck boards for the rails, one 8-ft. cedar 2x4 for the legs, and six 10-ft. cedar 1x4s for the slats and bottom boards. When you're at the home center, dig through the lumber piles to find the straightest boards with the fewest knots.

Build the Slatted Panels

Start by cutting the rails to length (A–D, Fig. A and Cutting List). Joint and square one edge, and then rip the rails to final width (Photo 1). Where possible, rip off any loose knots.

Rout a centered groove, 5/16 in. wide x 3/8 in. deep, on one edge of all the rails (Photo 2). Slightly chamfer the top edges of the bottom rails (but not the ends), to promote water runoff.

To make the slats, plane the 1x4s to 5/8 in. thickness and crosscut them into workable lengths. Joint one edge and then rip each length 3-5/16 in. wide.

Rout 5/16 in. x 5/16 in. rabbets on both edges to make the inside slats (E and Photo 3). Leave about 8 lineal feet with only one rabbeted edge, to make the end slats (F). The outer edge of each end slat is square. Because these slats go on opposite ends of the panel, the rabbets are on the front face on half of them and on the back face of the other half. Often, the 1x4s will have one good face and one not-so-good face. So, when you cut the end slats to final length, make

Start by ripping the rails to width from 5/4 cedar boards. This project is made with materials from the home center.

Rout a centered groove in one edge of each rail, to house the slats.

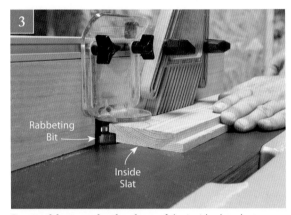

Rout rabbets on both edges of the inside slats, but on opposite faces, so the ends look like a "Z." The end slats are rabbeted on only one edge.

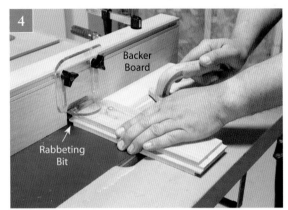

Rout tenons on the ends of each slat, using a rabbeting bit. Make one pass on each face. Use a backer board to guide the workpiece and prevent blowout.

sure that half of them are rabbeted on the "good" face and half are rabbeted on the "bad" face. This ensures that only the "good" faces will show on the completed planter. Cut all of the slats to final 9-7/8 in. length.

Use a rabbeting bit to rout centered 5/16 in. x 5/16 in. tenons on both ends of each slat (Photo 4). Adjust the bit's height and make test cuts on scrap stock to dial in the thickness; use the fence to set the length. Use a squarely-cut backer board with a screwed-on handle to support the workpiece and prevent blowing out the back edge.

Assemble each panel inside-face up. But before you start, mill a pile of 1/8 in. x 1 in. x 2 in. spacers. Lay the rails on a flat work surface. Then, starting with an end slat, slide each slat into position in the rails' grooves. Slip spacers between the slats at the top and the bottom. Install the remaining end slat to finish the job. Make sure both end slats are flush with the ends of the rails, that the assembly is

square, and that the inside faces of all the pieces are oriented correctly.

Remove the end slats, apply waterproof glue, and then glue them into the rails, flush with the ends. Make sure all of the internal slats are evenly spaced. Then nail them to the rails (Photo 5).

I used a BeadLOCK jig to drill the centered 7/8-in. deep mortises (Photo 6). Layout is simple. Just mark the midpoint of each mortise on each rail, 1-1/4 in. from the top edge on the top rails and 1-3/4 in. from the bottom edge on the bottom rails. The jig comes with shims that allow centering the mortises in stock of different thicknesses.

Use the offcuts from the 5/4 x 6 rails to make 1 in. x 1 in. ledgers (G) to support the planter's bottom boards (H). Glue and nail a ledger to the inside of both side panels, positioned at the height you want. You can mount the ledgers on the bottom rail and stack bricks to position the pots, or you can let the height of the pots or the amount of soil that you plan to use determine the ledgers' location.

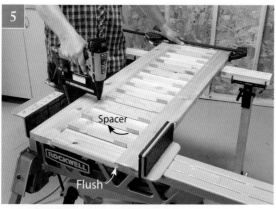

Assemble the panels. Spacers between the slats create uniform gaps. Glue the end slats flush with the ends of the rails. Nail the rest at the top and bottom.

Create mortises for loose tenons in the rails, using a BeadLOCK jig or other mortising tool. BeadLOCK tenon stock fits the unique mortises shown here.

Mark the legs for mortising by transferring the layout lines from the panels. Each leg will have mortises on two adjacent faces.

Glue and clamp the legs to the side panels. Swab glue in the mortises and on the ends of each panel. Install the BeadLOCK tenons; then install the legs.

Complete the planter by gluing the end panels between the assembled sides.

Apply an exterior stain to add color and protection from the rain and sun. Periodically reapply the stain to maintain the finish.

Make the Legs

Make the legs (J) by ripping a 40 in. length of 2x4 into two pieces that are 1-9/16 in. wide. Plane the sawn faces to square the stock. Then cut the legs to final length and round over all the edges.

Lay one of the panels on a flat surface and position one leg so it protrudes 3/4 in. at the panel's top and 1-1/8 in. at the bottom. Transfer the mortise layout marks from the panel to the leg. Then use the marked leg to transfer the layout lines to the other legs (Photo 7). Be sure to locate the mortises so that the legs' good sides will face out. Install the appropriate shims in the BeadLOCK jig to center the mortises, and then drill.

Figure A: Exploded View

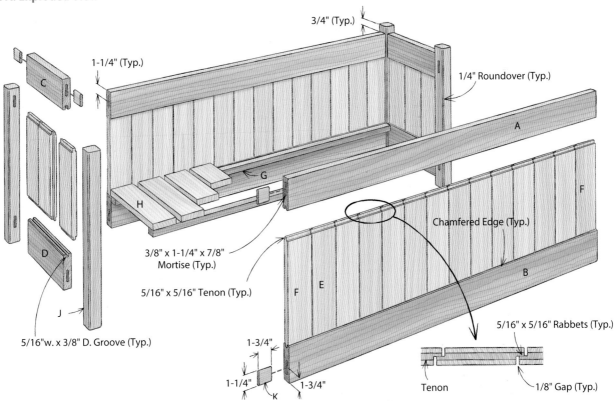

3/4" (Typ.)

1-1/4" (Typ.)

1/4" Roundover (Typ.)

C

A

G

H

Chamfered Edge (Typ.)

F

3/8" x 1-1/4" x 7/8"
Mortise (Typ.)

E

5/16" x 5/16" Tenon (Typ.)

F

D

B

J

5/16" x 5/16" Rabbets (Typ.)

5/16"w. x 3/8" D. Groove (Typ.)

1-3/4"

1-1/4"

1-3/4"

K

Tenon

1/8" Gap (Typ.)

Assemble and Finish

BeadLOCK supplies tenon stock that you simply cut to length to create the 1-3/4 in. long loose tenons (K). Miter one end of each tenon—the end that goes in the leg. Install the loose tenons when you glue and clamp the legs to the side panels (Photo 8). After the glue has set, repeat the process to glue and clamp the end panels between the side panels (Photo 9).

Apply the finish (Photo 10). I used a lightly pigmented exterior oil-based stain. The pigment provides a measure of UV protection, so the finish lasts longer.

Place the bottom boards on the ledgers, leaving 1/4 in. to 1/2 in. between them for drainage.

Line the planter with heavy-duty plastic, poke some drainage holes, and fill it with soil; this is the perfect setup for a miniature herb garden. Or skip the soil and create instant color by filling the planter with potted flowers.

Cutting List
Overall Dimensions: 47" L x 12-1/2" W x 18-1/8" T

Part	Name	Qty.	Material	Th x W x L
A	Side top rail	2	Cedar decking 5/4 x 6	1" x 3-1/4" x 44" (a)
B	Side bottom rail	2	Cedar decking 5/4 x 6	1" x 3-3/4" x 44" (a)
C	End top rail	2	Cedar decking 5/4 x 6	1" x 3-1/4" x 9-1/2" (a)
D	End bottom rail	2	Cedar decking 5/4 x 6	1" x 3-3/4" x 9-1/2" (a)
E	Inside slat	26	Cedar 1 x 4	5/8" x 3-5/16" x 9-7/8" (b, d)
F	End slat	8	Cedar 1 x 4	5/8" x 3-5/16" x 9-7/8" (c, d)
G	Ledger	2	Cedar decking 5/4 x 6	1" x 1" x 43-3/4"
H	Bottom boards	10	Cedar 1 x 4	3/4" x 3-1/2" x 9-5/8"
J	Leg	4	Cedar 2 x 4	1-1/2" x 1-1/2" x 18-1/8"
K	Tenons	16	BeadLOCK tenon stock	3/8" x 1-1/4" x 1-3/4" (e)

Notes:
(a) Rout a centered 5/16" w x 3/8" d groove in one edge.
(b) Rout 5/16" x 5/16" rabbets on both edges.
(c) Rout 5/16" x 5/16" rabbet on one edge.
(d) Rout 5/16" x 5/16" tenons on both ends.
(e) Miter one end of each loose tenon.

ART DIRECTION: VERN JOHNSON • PHOTOGRAPHY: LEAD PHOTOS: MIKE HABERMANN, ALL OTHERS, STAFF • ILLUSTRATION: FRANK ROHRBACH • WATERCOLOR: DONNA WHITMAN

by TIM JOHNSON

Nine-Pot Plant Stand

NO COMPLICATED JOINERY, JUST GLUE AND SCREWS

This sturdy little stand is perfect for your deck or patio. It's got room for your favorite plants and it doesn't take up a lot of space. When the weather gets cold, you can easily bring it, and a bit of summertime, indoors.

There's no complicated joinery, just glue and screws. The legs simply chase each other around the base, like a pinwheel. The arms follow suit,

but they're offset, so your plants have plenty of room to grow.

Once you make templates for the legs and arms and the jig for routing the discs, you'll have the stand together in no time. For tools, you'll need a tablesaw, jigsaw, router and a drill, plus clamps and a file or rasp. If you use construction-grade lumber, you won't need a planer or jointer. Rip the 1-1/2-in.-square column from a straight, clear 2x4 and use 1x stock for everything else. We went whole-hog, making ours out of mahogany. We spent about $100 for rough stock and milled it ourselves.

How to Build It

1. Mill all the parts to thickness. Cut the column (A), legs (B) and arms (E) to their finished dimensions.
2. Make templates for the leg and arm profiles (Fig. C).
3. Rough out the legs and arms with a jigsaw or bandsaw, about 1/8-in. oversize. Smooth the profiles with a rasp and sandpaper, a sanding drum mounted in your drill press, or an oscillating spindle sander.
4. Position each leg on the column and drill pilot holes for the screws (Photo 1). Be sure to mark the legs so they'll go back on the same column face during final assembly.
5. Round over the edges of the legs, except for portions that support the discs or go against the column (Fig. A). On the column, stop the round-overs 1-in. away from the joints.
6. Fasten the legs to the column with weatherproof glue and stainless steel screws.
7. Attach the column support block (C).

8. Glue the triangular-shaped arm blocks (D), cut from your leftover column stock, to the column (Photo 2). If a stuck-on block keeps sliding down the column, pull it off, remove the excess glue and stick it back on. Before gluing on the second pair, plane the first pair flush.

9. Attach the arms, following the same procedure you used for fastening the legs (Steps 4 through 6). Make sure the arms wrap around the column in the same direction as the legs, otherwise the discs won't be properly staggered.

10. Make a jig to rout the discs (Part F, Fig. A and Photo 3), cut them to rough size and rout them (Fig. B). Then round over the edges.

11. On all discs but one, drill out both holes left by the jig for the mounting screws. Countersink the holes on one side. Drill out only the center hole on the disc that'll go on top of the column. Position the discs on the legs and arms, drill pilot holes, and fasten them.

12. To keep your plants from getting blown off their discs by the wind, you may want to install pot spikes (G) in the arms and legs (Fig. A, Detail 1). Drill out the discs' center holes, as well as the corresponding screw holes in the legs and arms, with a 3/8-in. bit. Then glue sharpened mahogany or white oak dowels into the arms and legs. Slip the discs over the dowels and fasten them with the remaining screws. Stake your plants on the dowels, using the drainage hole in the bottom of the pot. Provide air space between the pot and the disc by using a plastic "deck protector" (available at garden stores).

Shopping List

6 lin. ft. of rough-sawn, 2-in.-square leg stock
12 bd. ft. of 4/4 stock
Optional construction-grade materials:
One 2x4x6 ft., clear red cedar
One 1x12x12 ft., clear red cedar
Thirty-two #12 x 1-1/4-in. FH stainless steel screws
Two #12 x 2-in. FH stainless steel screws
Weatherproof glue
5 lin. ft. of 3/8-in. white oak or mahogany dowel rod, for pot spikes (optional).

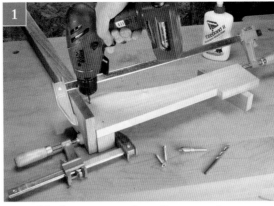

A stop block ensures perfect alignment when you mount the legs. First, clamp the stop block to the column. Then, clamp the leg to the stop block, making sure the bottoms of the leg and column are flush. After drilling pilot holes, countersink and drill out the leg holes so the screws will slip through and fit flush.

Glue the arm support blocks to the column, two at a time. Keep them properly aligned by going easy on the glue and using finger pressure to initially set the joint. Wait until the blocks are firmly attached before clamping. Once installed, these four triangular blocks create a mount for the arms that's offset from the legs.

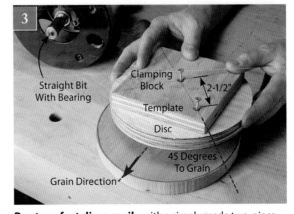

Rout perfect discs easily with a simply made two-piece jig. The block allows you to clamp the assembly to your workbench. The template lets you rout the round shape. Orient the screws at a 45-degree angle to the disc's grain. Then the disc will be fully supported across the grain when it's mounted.

Figure A: Exploded View

The legs and arms are offset to stagger the pots and maximize growing room for your plants.

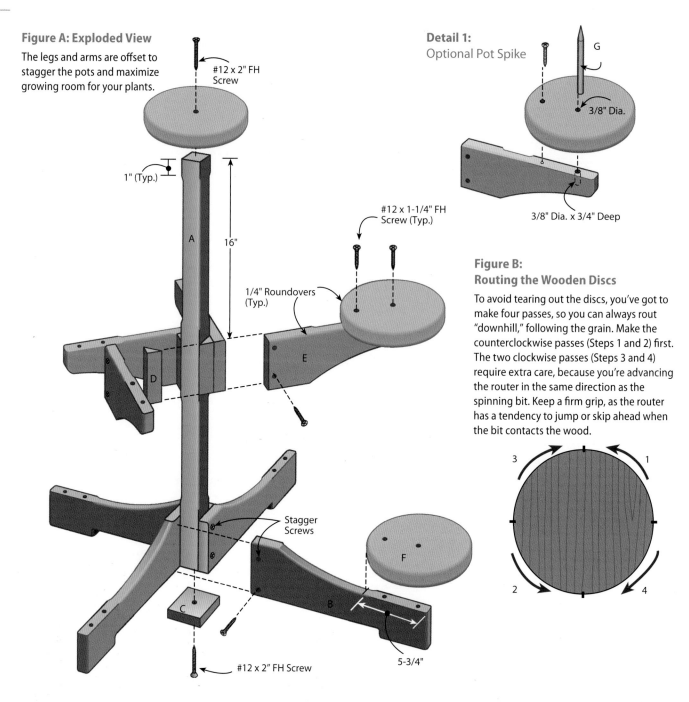

#12 x 2" FH Screw

1" (Typ.)

A

16"

#12 x 1-1/4" FH Screw (Typ.)

1/4" Roundovers (Typ.)

E

D

Stagger Screws

F

C

B

5-3/4"

#12 x 2" FH Screw

Detail 1:
Optional Pot Spike

G

3/8" Dia.

3/8" Dia. x 3/4" Deep

Figure B:
Routing the Wooden Discs

To avoid tearing out the discs, you've got to make four passes, so you can always rout "downhill," following the grain. Make the counterclockwise passes (Steps 1 and 2) first. The two clockwise passes (Steps 3 and 4) require extra care, because you're advancing the router in the same direction as the spinning bit. Keep a firm grip, as the router has a tendency to jump or skip ahead when the bit contacts the wood.

3   1

2   4

Figure C: Leg and Arm Profiles

The legs and arms share the same curve, so you really only have to make one template. Enlarge this pattern at a copy center by 250 percent and then again by 202 percent, until the dimensions are correct.

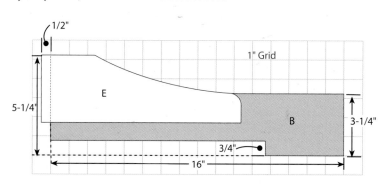

1/2"

1" Grid

E

5-1/4"

B

3-1/4"

3/4"

16"

Cutting List
Overall Dimensions: 33-1/2 x 33-1/2 x 36

Part	Description	Qty.	Dimensions
A	Column	1	1-1/2 x 1-1/2 x 34-1/2
B	Legs	4	3/4 x 5-1/4 x 16
C	Column Block	1	3/4 x 2 x 2
D	Arm Blocks	4	3/4 x 1-1/2* x 3-1/2
E	Arms	4	3/4 x 3-1/2 x 11
F	Discs	9	7-1/4-in. diameter
G	Optional Pot Spikes	9	3/8-in. dowel, 6-in. long

*Width of hypotenuse

by TIM JOHNSON

Shingled Patio Planter

JOIN IT WITH BISCUITS, OR CHOOSE NAILS

I f you can build a box, you can build this planter. It's much sturdier than most commercial versions, so it should last for many years. It's also the perfect opportunity for you to try your hand at shingling!

The opening accommodates a 30-in. drop-in plastic window-box planter. They're available at any garden store in several lengths. You could easily alter the design to fit a different-size box, or to accommodate individual pots. A square version of this planter would also look great.

All the materials you need lie waiting at a full-service lumberyard. You don't have to be choosy about the CDX exterior-grade plywood, but it pays to look through the cedar stock for straight, knot-free boards. If you invest in a bundle of top-grade red cedar shingles, you'll easily have enough to cover two planters. Lower grade bundles cost half as much, but have lots of knotty pieces that you won't use.

We cleaned up the 2x6 stock and 5/4 decking with a jointer and planer and cut all the pieces to size on a tablesaw. We used a bandsaw to cut the wide bevels on the top pieces, and a biscuit cutter and biscuits to reinforce the top's miter joints.

However, you can make a simpler version of this planter without having a shop full of tools. Except for the wide bevels, all of the cuts can be made with a circular saw and a 10-in. miter saw. Just make the top out of thinner stock and leave it flat (substitute 7/8-in.-thick cedar siding, the stuff with one rough and one smooth side, for the top and the legs). You don't have to use biscuits in the miters. Keep the pieces aligned by

pin-nailing the corners and let the weatherproof glue hold the joint. A drill, hammer and clamps complete the gotta-have tool list.

How to Build It

1. Cut plywood box pieces to size.
2. Assemble the box. Exterior-grade plywood is often twisted, so clamp the ends (A) between the sides (B) to help get all the edges flush. Fasten one corner at a time and drill pilot holes before driving the screws.

ART DIRECTION: VERN JOHNSON • PHOTOGRAPHY: LEAD PHOTOS: MIKE HABERMANN, ALL OTHERS, STAFF • ILLUSTRATION: FRANK ROHRBACH • WATERCOLOR: DONNA WHITMAN

Fasten the legs with the box upside-down. Keep the legs flush with the top of the box, and the planter will sit square. Apply glue and hold the leg with a clamp so it doesn't slip when you drive the screw. Flip the assembly over and install another screw near the top. Remove the clamp and move on to the next leg.

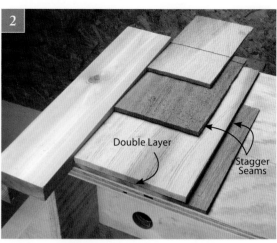

Install the shingles in four courses. Lay the second course directly on top of the first, so there's enough pitch to make water run off. Stagger the seams from course to course, so water won't seep in behind. Locate nails or staples so they'll be covered.

Cut stacked slots for biscuits, to reinforce the miter joints. Use a spacer to lift the second slot above the first.

Glue the mitered top on a flat surface. Draw the joints together by alternately adjusting the pressure on the three clamps. Waxed paper keeps the top from gluing itself to your bench!

3. Square up the box by installing the bottom (C).

4. Glue the L-shaped legs (D and E) together. Square the ends and trim them to 14-in. final length.

5. Fasten the legs to the box (Photo 1).

6. To match the scale of the planter, the shingles (F) have to be made smaller. Shorten them all to 8 in., measuring from the thin edge, except for the second course, which runs full length (Photo 2). Trim the shingles to width as you go and stagger the seams. Keep the fasteners covered—those on the last course are protected by the overhanging top.

7. Mill the top pieces (G and H, Fig. A). Clean up the wide bevels by sanding or planing, after cutting them on the table- or bandsaw.

8. Measure under the rim of your plastic planter to determine the correct size for the opening in the top. Make adjustments to the dimensions given in the Cutting List and Fig. A, if necessary.

9. Cut the miters. Measure from the inside edges. Make sure both pairs of pieces (sides and ends) are the same length.

10. Reinforce the miter joints with #20 biscuits (Photo 3).

11. Glue up the top (Photo 4).

12. Add cleats (J) and install the top.

Figure A: Exploded View

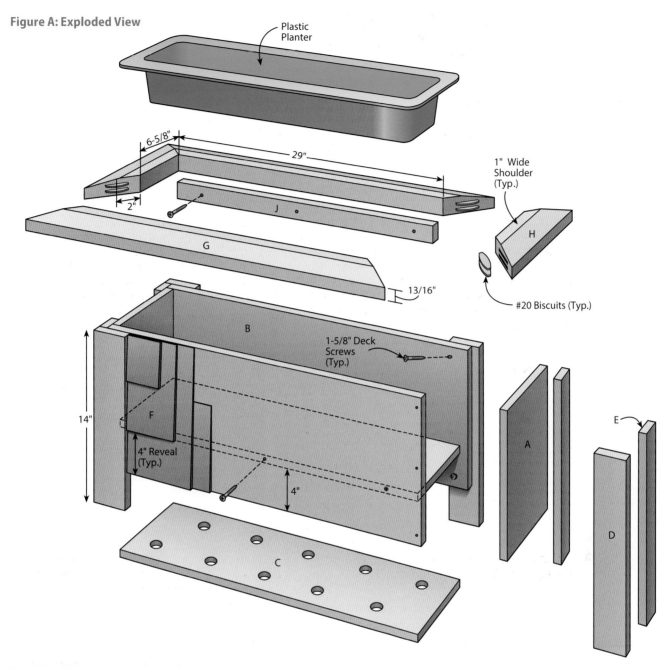

Plastic Planter

6-5/8"

29"

2"

J

G

1" Wide Shoulder (Typ.)

H

#20 Biscuits (Typ.)

13/16"

B

1-5/8" Deck Screws (Typ.)

14"

F

4" Reveal (Typ.)

4"

A

E

D

C

Shopping List

One 6-in. x 30-in. plastic window-box planter
One half-sheet (4x4) 3/4-in.-exterior-grade ply
One bundle of 16-in. #1 red cedar shingles
12 lin. ft. of 2x6 red cedar
8 lin. ft. of 6-in.-wide 5/4 red cedar decking
One box #6 x 1-5/8-in. deck screws
Weatherproof glue.

Cutting List

Overall Dimensions: 13-1/8 x 35-1/2 x 15-3/8

Part	Description	Qty.	Dimensions
A	Box Ends	2	3/4 x 8 x 11-3/4
B	Box Sides	2	3/4 x 11-3/4 x 30-1/2
C	Box Bottom	1	3/4 x 8 x 29-1/8
D	Leg Sides	4	7/8 x 3 x 15*
E	Leg Ends	4	7/8 x 1-1/8 x 15*
F	Shingles	many	Cut to fit
G	Top Sides	2	1-3/8 x 3-1/4 x 38* #
H	Top Ends	2	1-3/8 x 3-1/4 x 15* +
J	Top Cleats	2	11/16 x 1-1/4 x 28

*Oversize rough length
Cut to 29-in. between miters
+ Cut to 6-5/8-in. between miters

by TIM JOHNSON

Vine Trellis

CAREFUL LAYOUT KEEPS MANY DADOES ALIGNED

Make any climbing plant happy with this 6-ft. tall, free-standing trellis. We used dadoes, glue and screws to fasten the slats because trellises take a beating each year when you tear off the old vines. We built our trellis from cypress, one of the longest-lasting outdoor woods. Ours was recycled from old water tanks. White oak would also be a good choice.

Marking the legs for the dadoes can be confusing, but if you follow our marking procedures (Photos 1 through 4), you can't mess up. Even with our easy-to-make jigs, routing 68 dadoes is noisy, dusty and tedious (Fig. B and Photo 5). But once they're done, the dadoes make assembly foolproof. There's only one angle to remember: Everything slopes 6 degrees.

You'll need an angled template, made with the miter gauge on your tablesaw, to make the dadoing jigs. You'll also need a router with a straight bit to cut the dadoes, and a drill with a slotted tip for all the screws. We used a jointer and planer to mill our parts to thickness, but they could also be ripped to size on a tablesaw. The slats are thin, so be sure to use a push stick.

Mark the bottoms of the legs. Bundle the legs together and mark the front and back faces as one pair and the two side faces as the other.

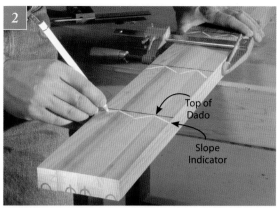

Mark the first pair of faces. The dadoes on the front and back faces match, so they can be marked at the same time. Arrange the legs with the triangles at the top. After aligning the ends, draw reference lines every 8 in. to mark the dadoes. Then go back and mark the slope, which runs outward from the center of each pair.

Top of Dado

Slope Indicator

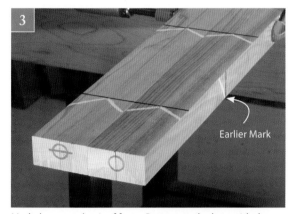

Mark the second pair of faces. Rearrange the legs with the circles at the top, and align the ends. Then mark the dadoes, using the same 8-in. spacing. This time, however, start 4 in. from the bottom. As you can see from the mark on the right, these dadoes are offset from the other pair of faces.

Earlier Mark

Your bundle should look like this. Check to see that each leg has its two outside faces marked, that the marks are staggered, and that the slope of the dadoes is clearly indicated.

How to Build It

1. Mill the legs (A) to thickness and cut them to length.

2. Mark the leg dadoes (Photos 1 through 4). The sides of the trellis are tapered, so the dadoes are angled.

3. Cut an 84-degree angled template, about 10 in. long and at least 4 in. wide. Use it to set the fence angle on the dadoing jigs (Fig. B).

4. Dado the legs (Photo 5). One jig will slope the right direction for the 3/16-in. deep dadoes on one side of each leg. The mirror-image jig will be correct for the other side.

5. Mill slat material to thickness and rip it into lengths, slightly oversize in width. Then plane (or rip) the slats to fit the leg dadoes.

6. Cut the bottom and top slats (B through E) for all four sides to length, with a 6-degree bevel on both ends. You can cut the slats to length in pairs because opposite sides of the trellis are the same.

7. Frame the front and back faces of the trellis (Photo 6). Align the beveled ends of the slats with the edges of the legs and drill pilot holes. Then drill out the holes in the slats so the screws slip through. Apply glue and assemble.

8. Cut the internal slats (F) to fit, and fasten them, following the procedures in Steps 6 and 7.

9. Stand the assembled front and back faces back-to-back in an "A," and assemble the sides, following Steps 7 and 8.

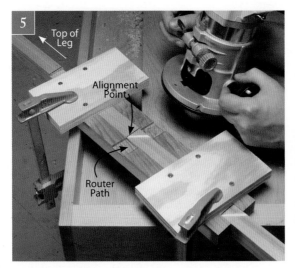

5 Top of Leg

Alignment Point

Router Path

6

Cut angled dadoes in the legs. Slide the leg in, top end first, making sure that its slope indicators run the same direction as the jig. Align the dado reference line on the leg with the top inside shoulder of the jig's dado, clamp and rout. Remember: the reference line always marks the top of the dado and the slope indicator should always be in the router's path.

Assemble one face at a time. Frame each face by fastening the top and bottom slats to a pair of legs. Then mark, cut and install the middle slats.

10. With a handsaw, square off the legs at the top of the trellis.

11. Bandsaw the spire (Part G, Fig. C). Lay out the pattern on two adjacent faces of a glued-up blank. Make the blank a foot long to keep your fingers a safe distance from the blade. After cutting the first two sides of the pyramid, tape the offcuts back onto the blank. Rotate the blank 90 degrees and cut the other two sides of the pyramid. Cut the second set of tapers the same way. After sanding, cut the spire from the blank.

12. Glue and screw retaining blocks (H) to the bottom of the spire, then soak it in preservative.

13. Screw the optional anchor spikes (Fig. A, Detail 1) onto the legs.

Cutting List
Overall Dimensions: 19 x 19 x 76

Part	Description	Qty.	Dimensions
A	Legs	4	1-1/8 x 1-1/8 x 72
B	Bottom slats, front and back	2	5/8 x 1-1/8 x 17-9/16*
C	Top slats, front and back	2	5/8 x 1-1/8 x 5-1/2*
D	Bottom slats, sides	2	5/8 x 1-1/8 x 18-1/2*
E	Top slats, sides	2	5/8 x 1-1/8 x 4-9/16*
F	Internal slats	26	5/8 x 1-1/8; cut to length*
G	Spire	1	3-1/2 x 3-1/2 x 5
H	Retaining blocks	4	1-1/8 x 1-1/8 x 1-1/4

* Ends cut at 84-degree angle; length is measured from long (lower) side.

Shopping List

35 lin. ft. (five 7-ft. lengths) of 1-1/2 x 1-1/2 stock
8 bd. ft. of 4/4 stock
Sixty-eight #10 x 1-1/4-in. RH brass screws (for the slats)
Four #8 x 1-3/4-in. FH stainless steel screws (for the spire)
Sixteen #10 x 1-in. FH stainless steel screws (for the optional aluminum spikes)
Weatherproof glue
8 lin. ft. of 1-in. aluminum L-angle (optional).

Figure B: Jigs for Routing Angled Dadoes

Because the sides taper, you need two mirror-image jigs, both angled 6 degrees from perpendicular. Use a template cut at 84 degrees to set the angle. Make the arms from extra leg stock. To get the proper spacing, slide another piece of extra leg stock between the arms when you mark the angles, fasten the fences and rout the dadoes. Use a spacer to keep the fences parallel so the dadoes are the same width on both jigs. The spacer's width depends on the diameter of the bit you use and the size of your router's baseplate. For example, to make the 1-1/8-in.-wide dadoes, using a 1/2-in. straight bit in a router with a 6-in. diameter base, the spacer is 6-5/8-in. wide.

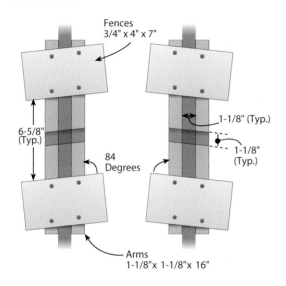

Fences
3/4" x 4" x 7"

6-5/8"
(Typ.)

84
Degrees

1-1/8" (Typ.)

1-1/8"
(Typ.)

Arms
1-1/8"x 1-1/8"x 16"

Figure C: Tapered Pyramidal Spire

The lower half of the spire continues the 6-degree taper of the sides. The top half accentuates the pyramidal shape. Ready-made spires, some with copper details, are also available at home centers and garden stores.

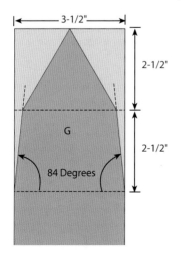

3-1/2"

2-1/2"

G

2-1/2"

84 Degrees

Figure A: Exploded View

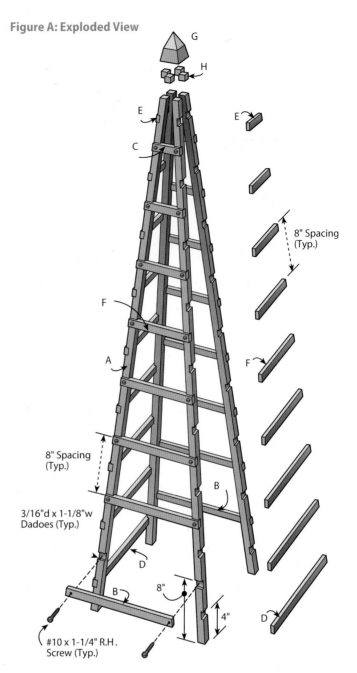

G

H

E

E

C

F

A

8" Spacing
(Typ.)

F

8" Spacing
(Typ.)

B

3/16"d x 1-1/8"w
Dadoes (Typ.)

D

B

8"

4"

D

#10 x 1-1/4" R.H.
Screw (Typ.)

Detail 1:
Optional Anchor Spikes

For windy conditions, you may want to anchor your trellis with aluminum spikes on each leg. For longer life, soak the ends of the legs in wood preservative or coat them with epoxy.

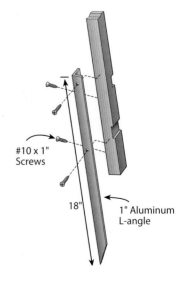

#10 x 1"
Screws

18"

1" Aluminum
L-angle

by TOM CASPAR

Planter Bench

THE PLANTERS AND BENCH ARE SEPARATE PARTS, ARRANGE THEM AS YOU LIKE

Smell the flowers. Touch the leaves. It's easy to enjoy plants when they're placed at a convenient height—and easier still when you can sit right next to them. Sitting on a planter bench brings nature close to hand.

While you can make this project with red cedar boards just as they come from the lumberyard, your planter bench will last longer and look better if you mill the wood first (see "Working with Red Cedar"). The joints will definitely be stronger because mating surfaces will be flat.

To build this project, you'll need about 17 1x6 deck boards 12' long and about four 2x4s 8' long. You'll also need some No. 8 deck screws (one box of 1-1/4" screws and one box of 1-5/8" screws) plus a bottle of water resistant glue suitable for outdoor projects.

By cutting the lumberyard boards to rough size first (Photos 1 and 2), you should be able to mill the deck boards to 7/8" thick and the 2x4s

to 1-1/4" thick. The exact thickness isn't really important, though.

Build the planters first. Start by making the corners (A and B). Cut the individual pieces to exact size, then glue them together. Mill the long panels (C) and short panels (D). Leave the short panels 1/4" extra-long. Glue and screw the long panels to the corners (Photo 3). Drill the pilot holes with a combination bit, counterboring the holes deep enough so the screws will penetrate at least 1/2" into the panels.

Measure the total length of one of the side assemblies, then trim the short panels to a length that makes the planter exactly square. Complete the box structure by adding the short panels. Run the short-panel screws at an angle, like toenailing a board.

Make the ledger strips (E and F) and glue them to the panels. Mill the top pieces (G). Miter them 1/2" longer than the total length of

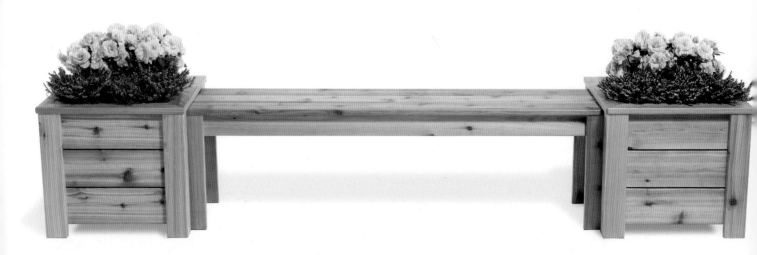

PHOTOGRAPHY-JASON ZENTNER • ILLUSTRATION-FRANK ROHRBACH

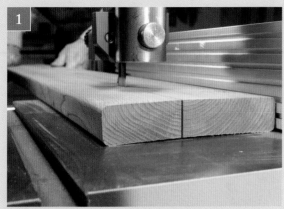

Rip warped boards on the bandsaw. This is much safer than cutting them on the tablesaw—there's no danger of kickback. To prevent a cupped board from rocking, put the concave side down.

Flatten each board on the jointer, then run it through the planer. Building a piece of outdoor furniture is much easier when you're working with flat stock.

Pre-drill holes for screws. Once red cedar is dry, it's very easy to split—particularly near the end of a board—if you don't pre-drill first.

Biscuit joints work well. These are the leg joints for the bench in this project. Once your pieces are flat and square, these joints can be made quite easily.

Working with Red Cedar

If you've ever built with red cedar, you probably know that most boards are cupped, bowed and twisted. That's not necessarily a problem for projects that are nailed or screwed together, such as fences and decks. But when it comes to making outdoor furniture with glued joints, warped boards won't do. You're better off treating those boards—smooth as they may be—as if they were rough lumber.

Before you start milling the wood, check its moisture content. It should be no more than 12%-14%. At that point, the wood has reached equilibrium with average outdoor humidity and has stopped cupping, bowing and twisting. (Although it will continue to move if it dries further.)

The first step in milling the wood is to cut your pieces to rough length. Group them in twos or threes—for example, to make two 12" pieces, cut a piece 25" long.

Rip the pieces to rough width (Photo 1). Look at the growth rings at the end of a board and make the cut nearest the center of the tree. This creates pieces that have the best chance of staying flat.

Flatten the pieces on a jointer (Photo 2) and run them through the planer. Joint one edge and rip them to exact width. Finally, crosscut to length.

Reinforce glued face joints with screws (Photo 3). Screws won't hold well in end grain, though. Make these joints with biscuits (Photo 4).

the box's sides, to create a 1/4" overhang all around. Cut the biscuit joints and glue the pieces with a band clamp.

Sand the planter base and top with 120 grit paper to make the joints flush. Screw the top to the base. Glue and screw the floor supports (H) to the base and make the floor boards (J).

Build the bench by starting with the legs (K and L). Glue the pieces together. Mill the long and short rails (M and N). Cut double biscuit slots in the ends of the long rails and in the legs (Photo 4). Use a 1/2" thick board under the plate joiner to space the slots. Cut more double biscuit slots in

the ends of the short rails and inside the long rails, again using the 1/2" spacer.

Glue the legs to the long rails. Reinforce these joints with screws (Fig. A). Complete the base by gluing the short rails between the long rails. Add the ledger pieces (P) and counterbore holes in them for fastening the seat. Mill the seat boards (Q) and install them.

Before you put on a finish, turn over the bench and planters and apply two or three coats of epoxy or waterproof glue to the ends of the legs and corners. Rot starts on end grain, but sealing these surfaces slows it down.

Figure A: Exploded View

Two #8 Deck Screws 1-1/4" L. Per Each End Panel (Typ.)

#20 Biscuit (Typ.)

Rail Is Inset 2-1/4"

Two #20 Biscuits, 1/2" Apart On Center (Typ.)

1/4" Overhang

#8 Deck Screw, 1-5/8" L. (Typ.)

1/8" Gap (Typ.)

Cutting List
Approx. Overall Dimensions: 18" H x 20" D x 8' L

Section	Part	Name	Qty.	Th x W x L
Planter	A	Narrow corner	8	7/8" x 2" x 17-1/4"
	B	Wide corner	8	7/8" x 3" x 17-1/4"
	C	Long panel	12	7/8" x 5-1/8" x 18"
	D	Short panel	12	7/8" x 5-1/8" x 16-1/4"
	E	Ledger	4	7/8" x 7/8" x 16-1/4"
	F	Ledger	4	7/8" x 7/8" x 14-3/8"
	G	Top	8	7/8" x 3" x 20-3/16"
	H	Floor support	4	1-1/4" x 1-1/4" x 16-1/4"
	J	Floor board	4	7/8" x 5-1/8" x 16-3/16"
Bench	K	Wide leg	4	7/8" x 3" x 16-1/4"
	L	Narrow leg	4	7/8" x 2" x 16-1/4"
	M	Long rail	2	1-1/4" x 3-1/4" x 56-1/4"
	N	Short rail	4	1-1/4" x 3-1/4" x 8-1/4"
	P	Ledger	4	1-1/4" x 1-1/4" x 8-1/4"
	Q	Seat	3	7/8" x 4-1/4" x 58"

This beautiful chest is designed to store the smaller outdoor amenities we use everyday, such as cushions for deck furniture, pool toys, or even gardening supplies. The cream-colored cypress is similar in appearance to a light-colored cedar or fir. Cypress is about 50 percent harder than clear cedar but about half the cost. Cypress is a rot-resistant member of the pine family native to swampy areas in the Southern United States. It's a stable wood, meaning it won't expand and contract a lot with the seasons. Cypress also machines well and takes any finish.

Built to Last in the Great Outdoors

The top sheds rainfall because the lid has a broad overhang and its hinge creates a gentle slope.

A chamfered bottom rail prevents rainwater from pooling and eventually causing decay.

Build the Legs and Rails

1. Sort your wood and select the best-looking pieces for the lid (A) and front panel (B). Rough-cut your stock according to the Cutting List, but leave everything oversize by at least 1/2-in. in length. Parts made from glued-up stock (G through L) should initially be cut an extra 1/2 in. wide.

2. Use a waterproof glue to face-glue three pieces of 3/4-in. stock for each leg (G). Glue up two pieces for the rail stock (H through L). Make an extra leg blank and an extra rail to test setups. Mark the best-looking face on each piece.

A deck-like bottom with gaps between the boards allows air to circulate to prevent mold or mildew. A galvanized metal screen called hardware cloth is mounted under the decking to keep unwanted critters out.

3. Trim the leg blanks to size after the glue has dried (Photo 1).

4. Lay out the groove location and the taper (Figs. B and C) on each leg. Position the legs on your bench just as they'll be on the chest to make sure you've got everything oriented correctly.

5. Cut the stopped grooves on each leg (Photo 2; Fig. B). It takes two fence settings to complete the two grooves. The first groove is cut with an outside face against the fence. The other groove is cut with the newly grooved edge against the fence. Be sure both grooves are equally set back on the legs.

6. Use a 1/2-in. chisel to square the corners where each routed groove ends.

7. Head to the drill press to cut the mortises (Photo 3; Fig. C). The mortise is really just a deeper part of the groove that accepts the tenon.

8. To finish machining the legs, cut the taper on the bandsaw. This can easily be done freehand. Use a 1/2-in. or wider blade and follow the line carefully. Sand the sawn surface smooth.

9. Now that the legs are finished, turn your attention to the rails. Lay out the tenons (Figs. D and E) on each end and cut them on the tablesaw. Use a test piece to check the fit of the tenons in the leg grooves. Shoot for a snug fit accomplished without a mallet.

10. Lay out and cut the tenon haunches on the bandsaw (Photo 4).

11. Dry-fit all the legs and rails to ensure all goes well at assembly. If a tenon bottoms out in the mortise before the joint is tight, trim 1/16-in. off the tenon length.

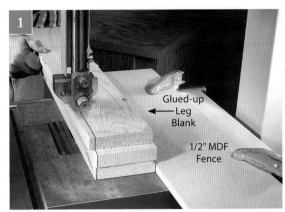

This entire project, even its stout legs, is built with rot-resistant cypress, a lightweight, weatherproof wood. To make the leg blanks, glue three pieces together and cut the stack on the bandsaw. Guide the cut with a 1/2-in.-tall fence that will contact only the bottom board.

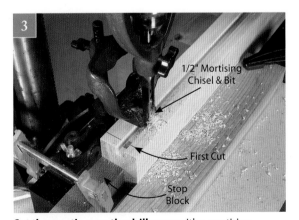

Rout stopped grooves on the legs to house the panels and the rail's tenons. The grooves are too long to use a stop block. Instead, mark where the groove ends on the edge of the leg. Make another mark on the router table across from the front of the bit. When the two marks meet, stop the router and remove the leg.

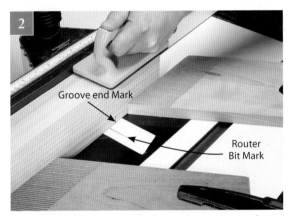

Cut the mortises on the drill press with a mortising attachment and a 1/2-in. chisel and bit. The groove guides the chisel so you don't get slightly staggered holes. A stop block ensures each mortise is the same distance from the end.

Figure A: Exploded View

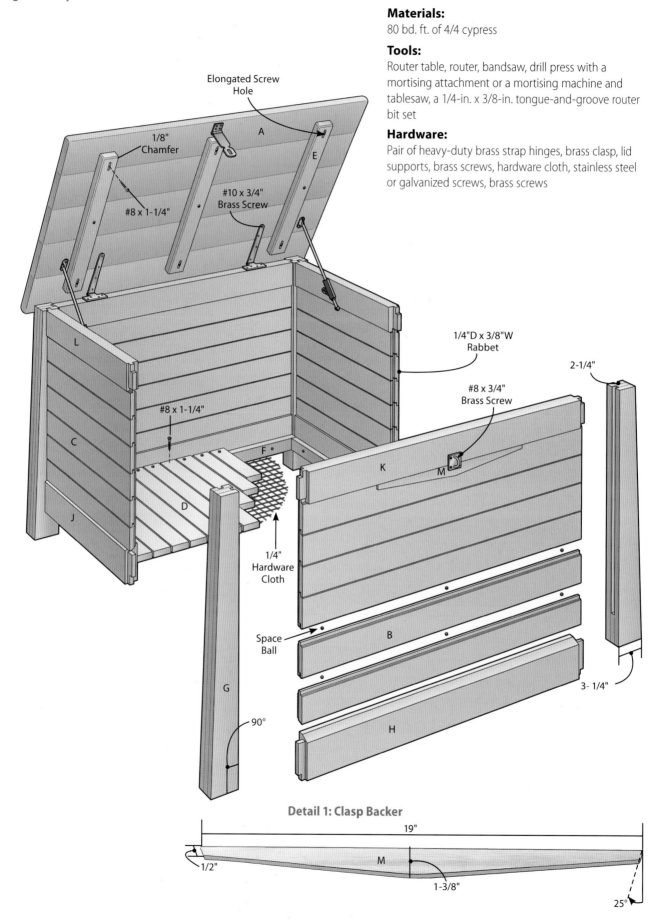

Materials:
80 bd. ft. of 4/4 cypress

Tools:
Router table, router, bandsaw, drill press with a mortising attachment or a mortising machine and tablesaw, a 1/4-in. x 3/8-in. tongue-and-groove router bit set

Hardware:
Pair of heavy-duty brass strap hinges, brass clasp, lid supports, brass screws, hardware cloth, stainless steel or galvanized screws, brass screws

Elongated Screw Hole

1/8" Chamfer

#8 x 1-1/4"

#10 x 3/4" Brass Screw

A

E

L

C

J

#8 x 1-1/4"

F

D

1/4"D x 3/8"W Rabbet

#8 x 3/4" Brass Screw

K

M

2-1/4"

1/4" Hardware Cloth

Space Ball

B

G

H

3- 1/4"

90°

Detail 1: Clasp Backer

19"

1/2"

M

1-3/8"

25°

Machine the Panels

12. Machine the tongue-and-groove joints in all the panel pieces (Photo 5; Fig. F).

13. Don't forget to machine the groove in the bottom of the upper rail (Fig. D) and to put a 30-degree bevel on each bottom panel board where it mates with the 30-degree bevel on the bottom rail (Fig. F).

14. On the tablesaw, shave 1/8 in. off the length of each tongue. This is necessary to make room for the Space Balls that fit between each tongue-and-groove panel board. Cypress is a stable wood, but it still moves, and these panels are trapped in their frames. Space Balls are like little rubber blueberries that keep an even gap between the boards but allow for seasonal expansion and contraction of the wood.

15. Cut rabbets on the ends of each panel board so they fit snugly into the leg grooves (Fig. F).

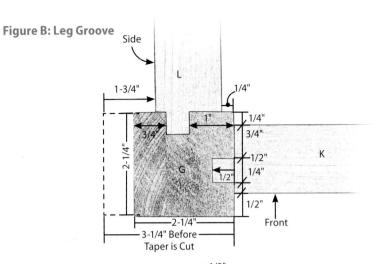

Figure B: Leg Groove

The rails have haunched tenons. The haunch fills the groove made on the router table and strengthens the joint by increasing the glue surface. Cut the tenons on the tablesaw; then bandsaw a notch to create the haunch on each tenon.

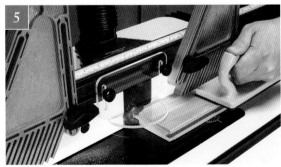

Cut the panel boards with a tongue-and-groove router bit set. Use a chamfer bit to ease the edges where the boards meet. Featherboards keep the stock flat on the table to ensure straight tongues and grooves.

Figure C: Mortise & Groove Placement

Figure D: Top Rail Tenon

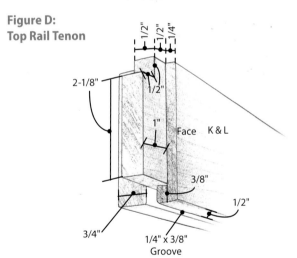

Figure E: Bottom Rail Tenon

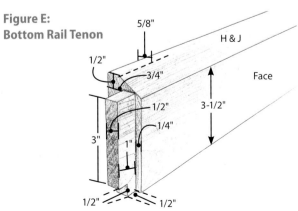

Assemble the chest upside down. Glue the top rail into one leg. Then stack the panel boards adding three or four Space Balls in each groove. Space Balls are little rubber balls that compress and expand to compensate for seasonal wood movement. Slip the bottom rail into the leg, add the second leg and clamp the assembly.

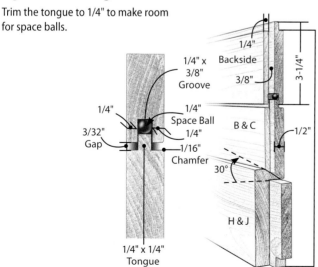

Screw down the decking using 1/4-in.-thick spacers to maintain even gaps. Hardware cloth is screwed to the bottom of the deck cleats to keep critters out of your chest, yet allow air circulation.

Figure F: Panel Tongue-and-Groove Joint

Trim the tongue to 1/4" to make room for space balls.

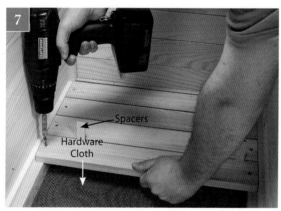

Assemble the Chest

16. Sand all the box parts through 120 grit.
17. Assemble the two end panels with waterproof glue and clamps (Photo 6).
18. After the two end panels are complete, assemble the rest of the chest in the same fashion. Set both front and back rails and panels into one end panel, add the second end panel and clamp. Be sure to check that your assembly is square.

Build the Lid

19. While the glue dries, edge-glue the boards for the lid. Take care to align each board flush. It's best to glue one board at a time for this operation.
20. Sand the top to 120 grit.
21. Cut the battens (E) and chamfer the outside edges (Fig. A).
22. Predrill countersunk holes in each batten on the drill press. **Note:** Be sure to elongate the screw holes on the ends of each batten to allow the lid to expand and contract (Fig. A).
23. Attach the battens to the lid with screws.

Install the Bottom

24. Cut the hardware cloth and screw it onto the bottom of the deck cleats.
25. Cut the deck cleats (F) and install them with screws along the bottom edge of the bottom rails (Fig. A).
26. Cut the decking (D) to fit. Predrill countersunk holes in the ends of each deck board and attach to the deck cleats (Photo 7).

Add the Hardware

27. Mount the hinges on the chest (Photo 8).
28. Glue the clasp backer (M) to the upper panel board and add the clasp (Fig. A, Detail 1).
29. Position and attach the lid closers.
30. I painted the bottom of each leg with a couple coats of two-part epoxy. This seals the leg ends and keeps them from wicking up any moisture. This is especially important if the chest sits on a concrete or brick patio.
31. You may choose to leave the wood raw. Cypress will age to a beautiful silver-gray color. If you want to preserve the color, look at some of the outdoor finishes designed for decks. Just remember, these finishes require frequent maintenance to keep their good looks. If you plan to put the chest in an enclosed porch, you're free to use your favorite finish.

Brass screw

Steel Screw

Mount the hinges with steel screws first. Then replace them with the brass screws. The steel screws pave the way, making it easier to drive the softer brass screws without breaking them.

Part	Name	Qty.	Dimensions
	**Cutting List**		
	*Overall Dimensions: 29" H x 44-1/2" W x 26-1/2" D*		
A	Lid	1	3/4" x 26-3/4" x 44-3/4"
B	Tongue-and-groove panel	12	3/4" x 3-3/8" x 36-3/4"
C	Tongue-and-groove panel	12	3/4" x 3-3/8" x 19-3/4"
D	Decking	12	3/4" x 2-3/4" x 19-1/2"
E	Lid batten	3	3/4" x 2" x 18"
F	Deck cleat	2	3/4" x 1-1/2" x 60"
G	Leg	4	2-1/4" x 3-1/4" x 28-1/4"
H	Bottom rail front and back	2	1-1/2" x 4" x 38"
J	Bottom rail side	2	1-1/2" x 4" x 21"
K	Top rail front and back	2	1-1/2" x 3" x 38"
L	Top rail side	2	1-1/2" x 3" x 21"
M	Clasp backer	1	1/4" x 1-3/8" x 19"

by THE EDITORS

Showcase Victorian Trellis

BUILD THIS EYE-CATCHING TRELLIS IN YOUR SHOP AND ASSEMBLE IT OUTSIDE JUST LIKE A KIT

Have you ever wanted to make an elaborate outdoor project without actually having to work outside? Our trellis is just the ticket: a summer delight you can build indoors.

Measuring 7 ft. wide by 9 ft. high, this spacious trellis is assembled in three sections. It can easily be built by one person, carried to the site and set in place. You don't have to dig post holes because the two seats make the trellis rigid enough to stand on its own.

Materials

We built our trellis of standard-size cedar lumber available at home centers. The backs of the seat sections are cut to size from factory-made diagonal cedar lattice sheets. When it came to the arches, we opted for the simplicity of cutting them from 3/4-in. AC exterior plywood rather than building them from solid wood. We painted the entire structure white to blend the cedar and plywood. White also contrasts nicely with the green of climbing vines..

You could use other materials to save some money and work. First, you could build the entire trellis from pressure-treated solid wood. Pressure-treated wood may not hold paint as well as cedar, however. Second, you could substitute white vinyl diagonal lattice sheets to avoid the hassle of painting cedar ones. Vinyl usually costs less than cedar sheets and is available at home centers.

Our trellis sits without anchors on a level, 8 x 10-ft. patio paver base. However, if you don't have a firm, level base on which to set your trellis, you may wish to extend the leg bottoms and anchor them in the soil with cement footings. If you do this, extend the leg bottoms and the footings to a point below the frost line in your area to prevent frost from pushing the structure out of level.

Get Going

Use the Shopping List to round up all the supplies you need at a home center, then follow Photos 1 through 11 to build this graceful addition to your yard.

Assemble the side lattice panels from cedar boards and clamp them to the legs. Drill pilot holes through the side panel, then fasten with 3-in. stainless steel decking screws.

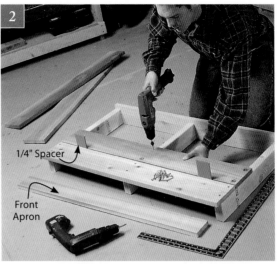

1/4" Spacer

Front Apron

Build the seat units from 2x4s and 1x6s. Use spacers to maintain an even 1/4-in. gap between the seat boards. Leave the front apron off for now.

Bolt the seat units to the trellis sides. You can easily get a socket wrench on the lag bolts with the front apron out of the way.

Add the top plate, cleats and lattice. Rout an ogee shape on the ends of the top plate before you attach it (see Fig. A, Detail 4).

Tips for Building the Trellis

- If you plan to put your trellis on a patio that isn't level, add an inch or two to the legs. Then trim them to fit the terrain, just as you would trim the legs of a wobbly chair.
- Drill pilot holes to avoid splitting the wood. It's possible to run screws into a soft wood like cedar without pre-drilling, but cracks often form later.
- •Assemble the larger pieces on a flat, level surface. This helps ensure that the assembled pieces end up square and accurately aligned.

If You Want a Natural Look...

You don't have to paint the trellis. If you prefer the look of natural wood, build the arches and curved side rails from cedar or treated lumber. Make each arch from two layers of curved pieces that are 3/4-in. thick and about 2-ft. long. Overlap the pieces in each layer for strength.

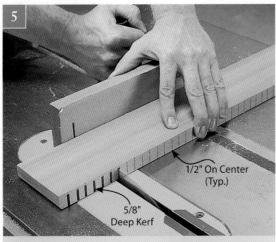

Caution: The saw guard and splitter must be removed for this operation. Be careful!

Cut saw kerfs in all the side rails that curve above the seats. Save straight-grained, knot-free wood for these pieces so they won't break when they're bent.

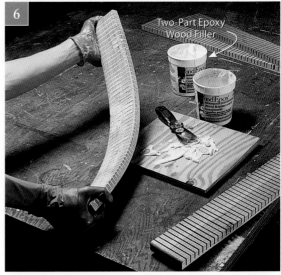

Fill the saw kerfs with a two-part epoxy wood filler. Then bend the side rails while the epoxy is flexible and insert them into the seat units. Let the epoxy dry with the rail in place.

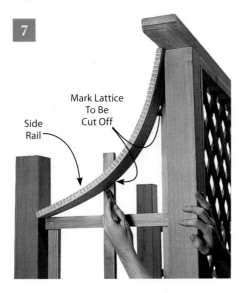

Mark the lattice for cutting and remove the hardened side rail. Cut the lattice with a handsaw and reinstall the side rail. Nail the side rail in place and remove the easily sanded excess filler with 80-grit sandpaper.

The curved side rails (Photo 7) are a little trickier to make as a bent lamination of solid wood. Re-saw 2x4s into 1/8-in.-thick strips. Bend the strips around a plywood form, glue with a water-resistant glue, and clamp.

Lay out the arches with a homemade compass. Cut them from two sheets of exterior plywood (see Fig. B). Then glue and screw the pieces together to make three sets of double-layer arches.

Smooth the edges with a belt sander. Then gang the three arches together and mark the locations of the arch bars (see Fig. A and Photo 10).

Finishing Your Trellis

Seal the bottom ends of the legs before screwing the arches to the seat units. Tip the seat units on their sides and liberally coat the bottom of the legs with thinned epoxy or polyurethane glue (see Oops!). Unsealed legs wick moisture from the ground, which may cause paint to peel around the base of the legs.

Sand all the rough surfaces and edges, and apply an oil-based primer, followed by two top coats of latex paint. Be sure to get good paint coverage on the cut plywood edges of the arches.

9

Place the arches on the arch bases, set on sawhorses. Hold the arches upright and accurately spaced using a clamped-in-place jig (Fig. C). Then drive 3-in. screws through the arch bases and into the arch ends.

Spacing Jig

Arch Base

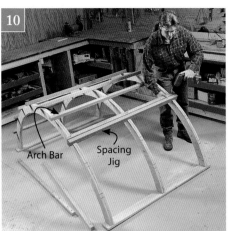

10

Mount the arch bars with 3-in. screws. Keep the arches accurately spaced and the overhang of the arch bars uniform by using the spacing jig. Now you've gone as far as you can in the shop. It's time to take the trellis outside.

Arch Bar

Spacing Jig

11 **Set the assembled arch in place** out in your yard, centered on the top plates. Shift the seat units until the arch bases line up with the top plates, then screw them together.

Arch Base

Top Plate

Oops!

We built our prototype trellis a few years ago. The roses look terrific but paint is peeling around the base of the legs and black spots are appearing around many screw heads. Rats!

Peeling Paint

The problem: Paint doesn't stick to damp wood. The ends of our legs soaked up rainwater like sponges, so the paint eventually peeled off.

The fix: We raised our trellis off the pavers and let the legs dry out. Then we filled the cracks with epoxy wood filler. We thinned some epoxy glue with acetone and brushed it on

the bottom of the legs to seal them. Polyurethane glue thinned with mineral spirits would work as well.

Paint Bleed-Through

The problem: The coated screws we used haven't rusted, but a chemical reaction has discolored the wood around them. Coated screws are fine for pressure-treated lumber, but they can stain cedar and redwood.

The fix: We replaced the coated screws with stainless steel screws. Then we repainted the trellis with Kilz stain-killing primer and applied two top coats of white paint.

Peeling Paint

Bleed-Through

Figure A: Victorian Trellis Details

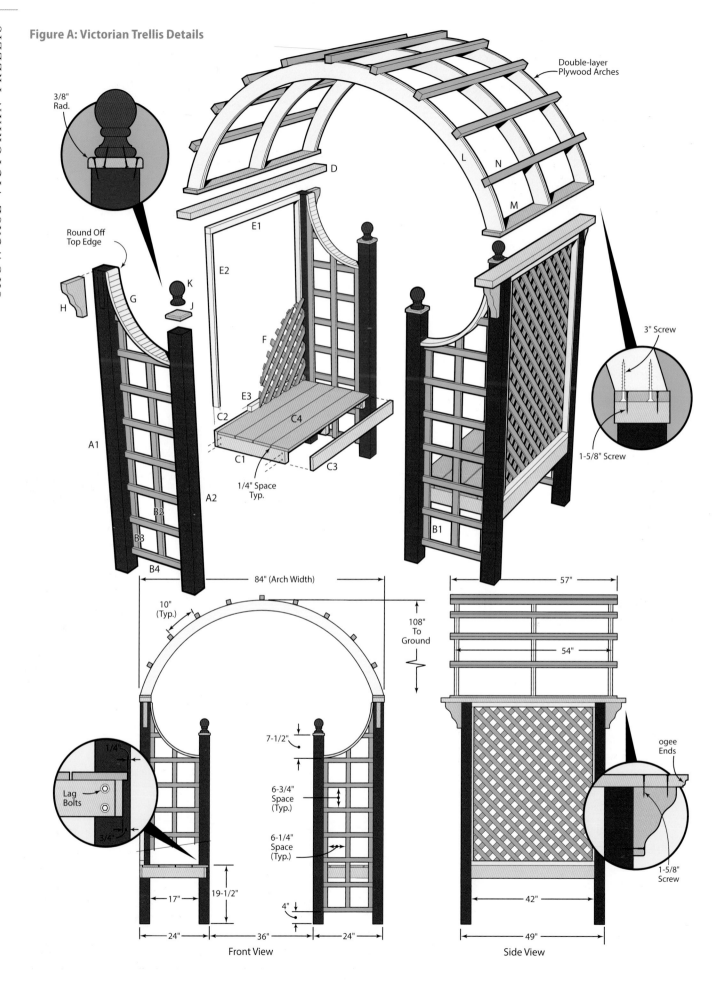

3/8"
Rad.

Round Off
Top Edge

H

G

K

J

A1

A2

B2

B3

B4

D

E1

E2

F

E3

C2

C1

C4

C3

1/4" Space
Typ.

Double-layer
Plywood Arches

L

N

M

3" Screw

1-5/8" Screw

B1

84" (Arch Width)

10"
(Typ.)

108"
To
Ground

1/4"

Lag
Bolts

3/4"

7-1/2"

6-3/4"
Space
(Typ.)

6-1/4"
Space
(Typ.)

17"

19-1/2"

24"

36"

24"

4"

Front View

57"

54"

ogee
Ends

1-5/8"
Screw

42"

49"

Side View

Figure B: Plywood Arch Layout

There's not enough room on one piece of plywood to make three full-length arches, so one of the arches must be laid out in two pieces. Cut out the two full-length arches first, then use one of them as a pattern for drawing the half-length arches.

Note: The ends of the half-length arch are different shapes! The ends that butt together are square, but the other ends are angled. Draw a layout line in the middle of a full-length arch before cutting it out, then transfer the line to one end of the half-length arch.

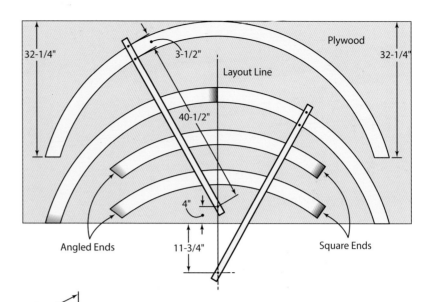

Figure C: Arch Spacing Jig

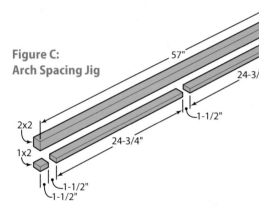

Materials List

4	4x4 x 12' cedar posts
2	2x6 x 8' cedar
2	2x4 x 8' cedar
7	2x2 x 8' cedar
6	1x6 x 8' cedar
18	1x4 x 8' cedar
	2-3/8" x 4' x 8' premade cedar lattice
	2-3/4" x 4' x 8' AC exterior plywood
4	3" cedar finial post balls
1 box	No. 6 x 1-1/4" stainless steel screws
1 box	No. 8 x 1-5/8" stainless steel screws
1 box	No. 10 x 3" stainless steel decking screws
10	3/8" x 3-1/2" lag bolts and washers
1 bottle	Water-resistant glue
A & B qrt.	Epoxy wood filler
1 gal.	Primer
1 gal	Paint

Cutting List
Victorian Trellis 9' H x 7' W x 4'1" D at base

	Part	Qty.	Name	Material	Length	Comments
End	A1	4	Tall Leg	4x4	73-1/2	
	A2	4	Short Leg	4x4	62-1/2	
	B1	4	Lattice Upright	1x4	51	Rip to 1-1/2" wide
	B2	4	Lattice Upright	1x4	58-1/2	Rip to 1-1/2" wide
	B3	4	Lattice Upright	1x4	69-1/2	Rip to 1-1/2" wide
	B4	32	Lattice Crosspiece	1x4	17	Rip to 1-1/2" wide
Seat	C1	6	Cleat	2x4	21-3/4	
	C2	2	Rear Apron	1x6	42	Rip to 4-1/4" wide
	C3	2	Front Apron	1x4	42	
	C4	8	Seat Board	1x6	42	
Trellis and Trim	D	2	Top Plate	2x6	63	
	E1	2	Upper Cleat	2x2	42	
	E2	4	Side Cleat	1x4	About 51	Rip to 1-1/2" wide, cut length to fit
	E3	2	Lower Cleat	2x2	42	
	F	2	Premade Lattice		42 x 54	
	G	4	Side Rail	1x4	27	Kerf-cut and bend
	H	4	Bracket	2x6	8-1/2	See Fig. A, Detail 4
	J	4	Cap	1x6	4" square	3/8" radius on top edges
	K	4	Finial	3" dia.		
Arch Assembly	L	3	Arch	3/4" AC ext. plywood	84	
	M	2	Arch Base	1x6	57	
	N	9	Arch Bar	2x2	57	

by TIM JOHNSON

Garden Arbor

AN ELEGANT STRUCTURE WITH SUPER-STRONG JOINERY

Here's a project that's guaranteed to add romance to your garden: an inviting gateway that promises beauty and tranquility to all who pass through.

Building this arbor is a big undertaking, because of its complex design and grand scale, but it isn't a difficult project. All the parts go together with simple joinery and basic tools.

The arbor's components are modular. You build them in your workshop and then assemble the arbor on site. The posts will stay straight because they're glued-together hollow boxes. These lightweight posts are much easier to lift and maneuver than solid posts. You'll create sturdy structures with strong joints by stacking and gluing pieces in layers. You'll fashion attractive curves and stylish ogees. Best of all, when you've found the perfect spot, I'll show you step by step how to install your arbor there.

I suggest that you build the arbor in No. 3 cedar. Omitting the gates saves $100. I built the Cadillac version you see here using D-grade cedar, which has very few knots. D-grade cedar is expensive and usually isn't available at home centers. I had to go to a full-service lumberyard to find it.

Knots are common in No. 3 cedar, so using it will make the arbor look more rustic. Knots also make No. 3 cedar harder to work with, so select boards with the fewest knots.

Cedar is sold as dimensional lumber (1x4, 1x6, etc.). I bought rough 1-in. stock. It comes with one side surfaced and is usually about 7/8 in. thick. I milled all my 1-in. cedar down to a 3/4-in. thickness by surfacing the rough side. The 2-in. cedar came surfaced on all four sides (S4S), milled to a 1-1/2-in. thickness. I cut off the rounded-over corners on the S4S cedar.

Build the Side Panels

The side panels (A, Fig. A) are three-layer sandwiches, with vertical pickets (A1 and A2) held between horizontal rails (A3 through A6). Assembly is easy because the pieces are simply stacked, glued and screwed. The top rail is three layers thick. Its inside rail covers the tops of the pickets to protect the end grain. The other rails are fastened to the outside, so moisture can drain between the pickets. Glue these panels together on a flat surface, so they aren't twisted. Use waterproof glue.

1. Cut all the pieces to width.
2. Cut the rails and the two outer pickets to length, with the ends squarely cut.
3. Make patterns for the curved profiles in the top rails (Fig. B) by swinging arcs on 1/4-in.-thick scrap stock and bandsawing. Use the patterns and reference points A and B to transfer the arcs to the top rail blanks (A3 and A4). Then saw out the rails.

Rail Position

Waterproof Glue

Outer Picket

The side panels are layered like a sandwich. Lay the outer pickets in position on top of the rails to make the frame. Apply glue and tack the pieces together with a pin nail in each corner. Square the frame by adjusting it until both diagonal measurements are the same. Then screw the stiles to the rails.

ART DIRECTION: DAVID SIMPSON & RICK DUPRE · PHOTOGRAPHY: EXTERIOR PHOTOS, SHAWN NIELSON; INTERIOR PHOTOS, RAMON MORENO · ILLUSTRATION: FRANK ROHRBACH

Figure A: Exploded View

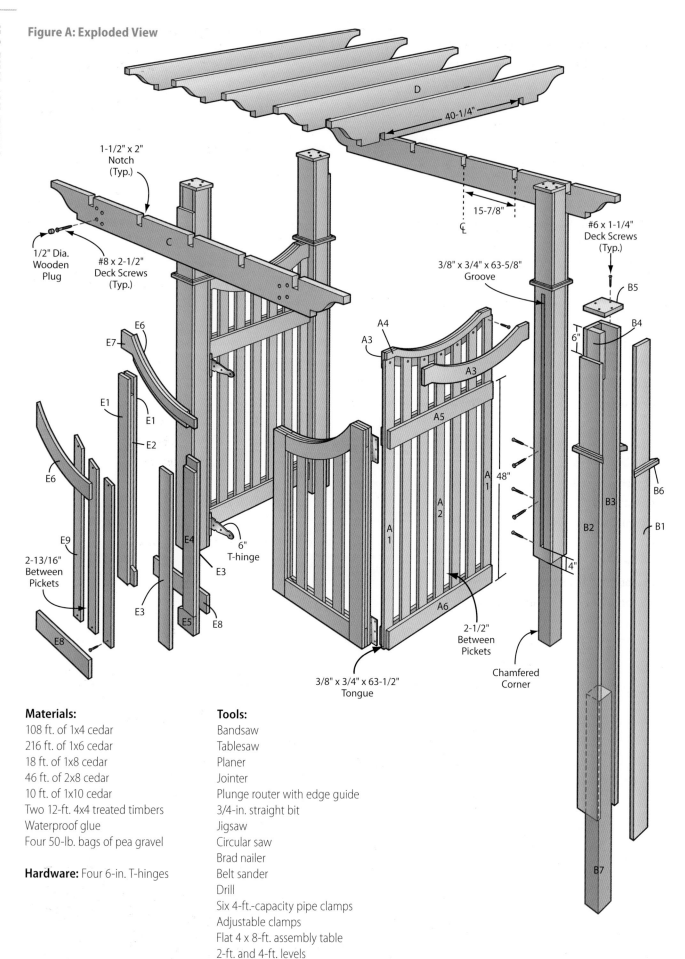

1-1/2" x 2"
Notch
(Typ.)

1/2" Dia.
Wooden
Plug

#8 x 2-1/2"
Deck Screws
(Typ.)

40-1/4"

15-7/8"

#6 x 1-1/4"
Deck Screws
(Typ.)

3/8" x 3/4" x 63-5/8"
Groove

6"

E6
E7
E1
E1
E2

E6

E9

2-13/16"
Between
Pickets

E8

E4

E3
E5
E8

E3

6"
T-hinge

3/8" x 3/4" x 63-1/2"
Tongue

2-1/2"
Between
Pickets

Chamfered
Corner

A4
A3
A3
A3
A5
A2
A1
A1
A1
A6

48"

4"

B5
B4
B3
B2
B1
B6
B7

C
D

Materials:
108 ft. of 1x4 cedar
216 ft. of 1x6 cedar
18 ft. of 1x8 cedar
46 ft. of 2x8 cedar
10 ft. of 1x10 cedar
Two 12-ft. 4x4 treated timbers
Waterproof glue
Four 50-lb. bags of pea gravel

Hardware: Four 6-in. T-hinges

Tools:
Bandsaw
Tablesaw
Planer
Jointer
Plunge router with edge guide
3/4-in. straight bit
Jigsaw
Circular saw
Brad nailer
Belt sander
Drill
Six 4-ft.-capacity pipe clamps
Adjustable clamps
Flat 4 x 8-ft. assembly table
2-ft. and 4-ft. levels

4. Glue and screw the inside top rail to one of the outside rails. Make sure the ends align and the glue joint is tight. Remove any squeezed-out glue.

5. Tack the frame together (Photo 1). The two outer pickets protrude beyond the rails by 3/8 in. to form tongues (Detail 1). Draw layout lines on these pickets to indicate the ends of the rails. Lay the pickets on the top and bottom rails. Butt the pickets against the inside top rail and align the other ends with the bottom edge of the bottom rail. Apply glue and tack the corners.

6. Square the frame and then screw it together with 1-1/4-in. deck screws. Drill countersunk pilot holes first, so the screws don't split the wood. Work fast, so you finish before the glue sets up.

7. Use your layout lines to attach one middle rail to the bottom side of the frame. Make sure its ends align with the top and bottom rails.

8. Install the inner pickets, using 2-1/2-in.-wide spacers (Photo 2). Cut the pickets to length as you go. Fasten them with glue and screws in predrilled holes.

9. Glue and clamp the remaining top, middle and bottom outside rails. Make sure the ends align.

10. Smooth the curve on the top rails using a belt sander or a sanding drum chucked in a drill.

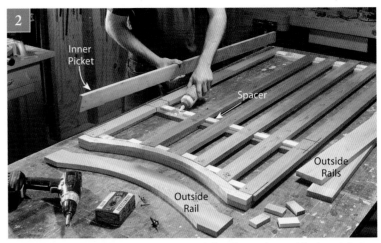

Position the inner pickets, using spacers, and then fasten them with glue and screws through predrilled holes. Remove the spacers and complete the side panel by gluing and clamping the outside rails.

Build the Posts

The posts (B) are hollow, made from four pieces that are simply butted, glued and clamped (Photo 3).

11. Cut the post pieces (B1 through B3) to width and length. The sides are narrower, so butting them between the front and back pieces creates a square post.

12. Glue and clamp the sides to the back piece. Remove any squeezed-out glue.

13. Glue and screw a block (B4) to the back side of the front piece.

Figure B: Layout for Side Panel Top Rails

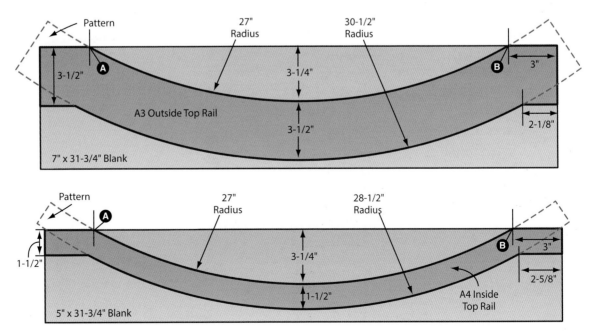

The posts are built as hollow boxes. They weigh a lot less than solid timbers and are more stable. The front piece is shorter, creating a ledge to support the arbor's horizontal beams. The attached screw block anchors the beam's mounting screws.

Rout a groove on each post's back face, sized to fit the protruding pickets on the side panels. Tongue-and-groove joints secure the side panels to the posts.

Glue each side panel between two posts. These end assemblies are about the same size as a 4x8 sheet of plywood, so before you glue, make sure you'll be able to move the glued-up assembly out of your shop.

14. Glue and clamp the front piece to complete the post; make sure the bottom edges are flush. Remove any squeezed-out glue.

15. Rout a stopped groove in the back of each post, centered and sized to fit the side panel's picket tongues (Photo 4). Square the bottom end of each groove 4 in. from the post's bottom edge.

Glue Up the End Assemblies

Each side panel mounts between two posts with tongue-and-groove joints (Photo 5). These end assemblies are large, so enlist a friend to help. Work on a flat surface, so you don't glue a twist into the assembly.

16. Lay the posts on top of three pipe clamps, spaced far enough apart for the side panel to fit between them. Position the clamps so they'll be right under the side panel rails.

17. Position the side panel between the posts. Set it on blocks, so the picket tongues align with the grooves.

18. Test-fit the joint. Add three clamps on top of the posts, directly over the panel rails, and slowly draw the joint together. Square the assembly by making sure the panel sits 4 in. from the bottom of each post. Apply even clamping pressure above and below each joint. The panel's rail shoulders should fit tightly against the posts.

19. Disassemble the joints, apply glue to the tongues and grooves and draw the assembly back together. Remove any squeezed-out glue. If gluing both tongue-and-groove joints at once is too nerve-wracking, glue one joint at a time.

Make the Beams and Rafters

The beams and rafters (C and D) lock together with half-lap joints. The notches have to be located precisely, so the assembled beams and rafters will fit properly around the posts at the top of the arbor.

20. Cut the beams and rafters to width and length.

21. Clamp the two beams together and lay out the two outer notches (Detail 2). Make sure the ends of the beams are flush. Otherwise, the notches won't line up correctly. Lay out the inner notches. They're evenly spaced between the outer notches.

22. Cut the notches using a circular saw, with the blade set to cut to the bottom of the notch (Photo 6). Use a chisel to clear the waste and smooth the bottom of the notches (Photo 7).

23. Gang the five rafters together and cut the notches in them the same way. The rafters have only two notches; they're 40-1/4 in. apart.

24. Make a pattern (Detail 2) and mark the ogee profiles on the beams and rafters. On the beams, the notches are at the top; on the rafters, the notches go at the bottom. Saw out the profiles (Photo 8).

Build the Gates

The gates (E) are layered, just like the side panels, but they go together differently and feature robust mortise-and-tenon joints.

25. Cut the hinge and latch stile components (E1 through E4) to length and width. Cut the loose tenons (E5) to size, too. The last 1-1/2 in. of their top edges slope 1 in. to shed moisture.

26. Glue the hinge and latch stiles by sandwiching an inside stile and a loose tenon between the outside stiles. Keep all the pieces aligned and the edges flush when you clamp. It helps to tack the pieces in place as you stack them together. After clamping, remove the squeezed-out glue—don't forget the bottom of the mortises. After gluing, you'll have three-layer stiles with flush edges, open mortises at the top and tenons protruding from the bottom.

27. Cut the bottom gate rails (E8) to width and length.

28. Make an arched pattern for the outside top gate rails (E6, Fig. C).

29. Cut blanks for the outside top gate rails. Cut the ends of these blanks at 70-degree angles, spaced 18-3/4 in. These angled top rail blanks must be the same length as the bottom rails.

30. Use reference points A and B on Fig. C to position your pattern on the blank. Transfer the arches and cut out the rail.

31. Make an arched pattern and cut the blank for the inside top gate rail (E7, Fig. C). This rail extends beyond the outside top rails to create

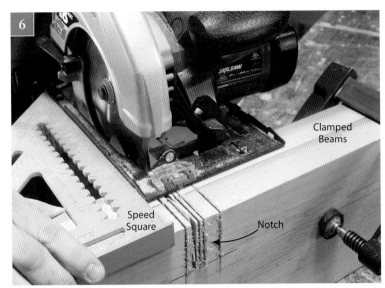

Cut notches in the beams and rafters. Clamping the pieces together allows you to cut perfectly aligned notches. Use a speed square to make straight cuts. Establish the shoulders first. Then make cuts in the middle until only thin pieces remain.

Clear the waste by twisting a chisel against the thin pieces. These pieces break out easily because of their short grain. After you've removed the waste, clean up the bottoms of the notches with your chisel.

Saw profiles on the ends of the beams and rafters. First, cut the curve. Then cut the straight shoulder. Hold the waste piece while you cut, so it doesn't tear away.

Glue the gate together. Apply glue, assemble the frame, square it and clamp the joints. The layered stiles and upper rail are glued together prior to assembly. After you install the pickets, glue and clamp the remaining top and bottom rails.

Anchor the arbor with treated 4x4s fastened inside the posts. This construction method assures long life, because treated lumber lasts much longer underground than cedar.

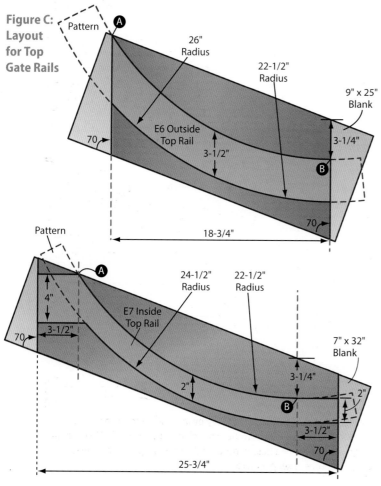

Figure C: Layout for Top Gate Rails

the tenons. Cut the ends of this blank at 70 degrees, spaced 25-3/4 in. This rail is as long as the gate is wide.

32. Use reference points A and B on Fig. C to position your pattern and transfer the arches. Establish the two tenons by extending lines at 90-degree angles from the edges. Cut out the inside top rail.

33. Glue the inside top rail to one of the outside rails.

34. Glue the gate frames together (Photo 9). Clamp one bottom rail between the stiles, under the protruding tenons. Apply glue inside the mortises at the top of the stiles and to the tenons on the two-layer top rail. Install the top rail. Make sure the gate is square. Clamp the mortise-and-tenon joints at the top and glue and screw the tenons to the bottom rail.

35. Install the pickets (E9), using spacers, and fasten them with glue and screws. Then glue and clamp the remaining top and bottom rails.

36. Seal the exposed end grain on the tops of the gates with epoxy or thinned waterproof glue.

Install the Arbor

37. Install the anchor posts (Photo 10). Treated timbers are never straight. So that they'll seat flush inside the hollow posts, joint adjacent faces of each 4x4 to create a flat, square corner. Rout a clearance chamfer to avoid hardened glue inside the post. Slide the 4x4 halfway into the hollow post, leaving 36 in. exposed, and fasten it to the inside corner with 2-1/2-in. deck screws on both sides (Detail 3). For longest life, orient the 4x4s so the "factory" ends go in the ground and the ends you've sawn go inside the posts.

38. Determine the arbor's position in your garden and dig 8-in.-dia. x 40-in.-deep holes for the posts. First, drive a stake to mark the center of each hole. Establish the holes by spading down about 6 in. on all four sides of the stake. Then go to town with a post-hole digger. Using a level, determine the ground's slope and mark the hole that sits at the highest grade.

39. Install the first end assembly (Photo 11). Plumb the post that goes in the hole at the highest grade (Photo 12). Starting with this

Slip one end assembly into the holes you've dug. Even though this assembly is huge, it's easy to maneuver, because it doesn't weigh much and isn't top-heavy.

Plumb the first post. Raise the end assembly on blocks, so the bottom edges of the cedar rest a couple inches above the ground. Stake the post in position, using a level and a diagonal brace.

Level the assembly with shims. Then plumb the second post and stake it in position, using a second diagonal brace. With this end assembly plum, level and staked, you're ready to install the other one.

Install the second end assembly on blocks and level it with the first, side to side and front to back. You'll need two levels, a pair of long, straight boards and more shims.

Plumb the second end assembly by fastening it to the first with braces top and bottom, each cut to match the arbor's width. Measure the diagonals and make adjustments until the base is square. Then install a diagonal brace to keep it there.

Clamp the beams in position by replacing the upper braces one at a time. Rest the beam on the posts' built-in ledges. Align the notches with the side of the posts.

Install the outside rafters. Supported by the half-lap joints, they nest against the sides of the posts. Install the inside rafters last.

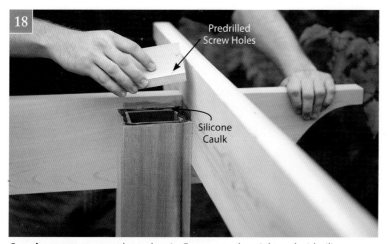

Cap the posts to cover the end grain. Form a weather-tight seal with silicone caulk. Fasten the caps with screws. Left unprotected, end grain wicks moisture, which accelerates decay.

Fill the post holes with pea gravel. It's much easier to use than concrete and less messy. Tamp the gravel around the posts to securely anchor the structure.

Install trim with galvanized pin nails and waterproof glue. Countersink the nails and fill the holes with exterior-grade putty, so you don't end up with black stains from contact between metal and moisture.

Install the gates. Clamp them flush with the back faces of the posts, using shims at all four hinge locations to establish even gaps all around. Then screw on the hinges.

Detail 1: Side Panel Tongue

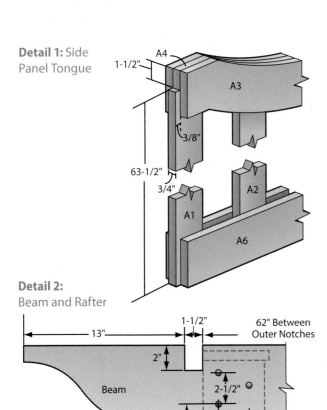

1-1/2"
A4
A3
63-1/2"
3/8"
3/4"
A1
A2
A6

Detail 2: Beam and Rafter

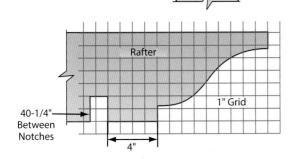

13"
1-1/2"
62" Between Outer Notches
2"
Beam
2-1/2"
2-1/2"
5-1/2"
2-1/4"
1-1/2"
Post

Rafter
1" Grid
40-1/4" Between Notches
4"

Detail 3: Post End View

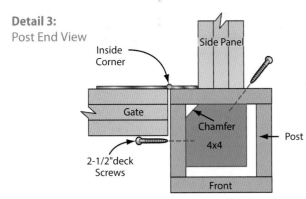

Side Panel
Inside Corner
Gate
Chamfer
4x4
Post
2-1/2" deck Screws
Front

Detail 4: Trim Dimensions

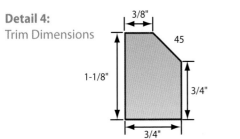

3/8"
45
1-1/8"
3/4"
3/4"

---

post assures that all four posts will be above grade. When the first post is staked in position, level the assembly front to back (Photo 13). Then plumb the second post.

40. Use this staked assembly to install the other end assembly level, plumb and square (Photos 14 and 15).

41. Install the beams and rafters (Photos 16 and 17). Fasten them to the posts with screws and plugs.

42. Screw on the post caps after sealing the joints with silicone caulk (B5, Photo 18).

43. Fill and tamp the post holes (Photo 19).

44. Make and install the post trim (Photo 20).

45. Install the gates (Photo 21). Make sure the gap between the gates is large enough, at least 1/4-in., so they swing freely. Install a latch to close the gates. I used a large hook and eye screw combination mounted on the back of the gates for appearance. To hold the gates open, I installed a second hook to one side panel and a second eye screw to the other.

46. If you want to maintain the look of the fresh cedar, apply a finish. I used Penofin's Western Red Cedar exterior stain. You should plan to recoat any exterior finish biennially. Without finish, the cedar will weather to gray within one or two seasons.

Cutting List

Overall Dimensions: 91"W x 69-1/4"D x 96"H (footprint: 41-3/4" x 62")

Part	Name	No.	Stock	Final Dimension
A	Side panel	2		2-1/4" x 32-1/2" x 65"
A1	Outer pickets	4	1x4	3/4" x 2-1/2" x 63-1/2"
A2	Inner pickets	10	1x4	3/4" x 2-1/2" x 63"*
A3	Outside top rail	4	1x8	3/4" x 6-3/4" x 31-3/4"
A4	Inside top rail	2	1x6	3/4" x 4-3/4" x 31-3/4"
A5	Middle rail	4	1x6	3/4" x 3-1/2" x 31-3/4"
A6	Bottom rail	4	1x6	3/4" x 4" x 31-3/4"
B	Post	4		5" x 5" x 92"
B1	Side	8	1x6	3/4" x 3-1/2" x 92"
B2	Front	4	1x6	3/4" x 5" x 86"
B3	Back	4	1x6	3/4" x 5" x 92"
B4	Screw block	4	2x8	1-1/2" x 3-1/2" x 10"
B5	Cap	4	1x6	3/4" x 4-1/2" x 5-1/4"
B6	Trim	16	1x4	3/4" x 1-1/8" x 6-1/2"
B7	Anchor	4	4x4**	3-1/4" x 3-1/4" x 72"
C	Beam	2	2x8	1-1/2" x 7" x 91"
D	Rafter	5	2x8	1-1/2" x 7" x 69-1/4"
E	Gate	2		2-1/4" x 25-3/4" x 48"
E1	Outside hinge stile	4	1x6	3/4" x 3-1/2" x 48"
E2	Inside hinge stile	2	1x6	3/4" x 3-1/2" x 40"
E3	Outside latch stile	4	1x6	3/4" x 3-1/2" x 38"
E4	Inside latch stile	2	1x6	3/4" x 3-1/2" x 32"
E5	Loose tenon	4	1x6	3/4" x 4" x 5"
E6	Outside top gate rail	4	1x10	3/4" x 8" x 18-3/4"
E7	Inside top gate rail	2	1x8	3/4" x 7" x 25-3/4"
E8	Bottom gate rail	4	1x6	3/4" x 4" x 18-3/4"
E9	Gate pickets	6	1x4	3/4" x 2-1/2" x 42"*

*cut to length **treated

Note: Page numbers in *italics* indicate projects.

More Great Books from Fox Chapel Publishing

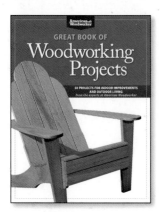

**Great Book of
Woodworking Projects**
ISBN 978-1-56523-504-5 **$24.95**

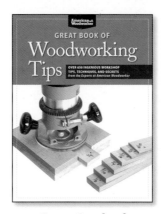

**Great Book of
Woodworking Tips**
ISBN 978-1-56523-596-0 **$24.95**

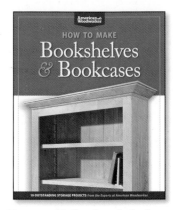

**How to Make Bookshelves
& Bookcases**
ISBN 978-1-56523-458-1 **$19.95**

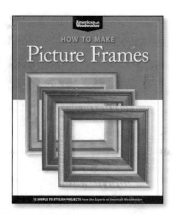

How to Make Picture Frames
ISBN 978-1-56523-459-8 **$19.95**

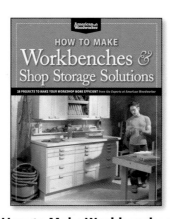

**How to Make Workbenches
& Shop Storage Solutions**
ISBN 978-1-56523-595-3 **$24.95**

How to Make Kitchen Cabinets
ISBN 978-1-56523-506-9 **$24.95**

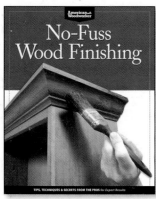

No-Fuss Wood Finishing
ISBN 978-1-56523-747-6 **$19.99**

Great Book of Wooden Toys
ISBN 978-1-56523-431-4 **$19.95**

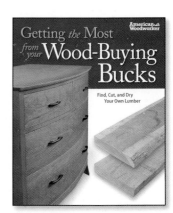

**Getting the Most from your
Wood-Buying Bucks**
ISBN 978-1-56523-460-4 **$19.95**